Parents' Guide to
IQ TESTING
and GIFTED
EDUCATION

*All you need to know to make
the right decisions for your child*

With a Special Section on
Bright Kids with Learning Problems

David Palmer, Ph.D.

Parent Guide Books
Long Beach, California

For more information contact:
Parent Guide Books
PO BOX 8403
Long Beach, Ca. 90808-8403

Or visit: www.parentguidebooks.com

Cover/Interior design: Irene Archer, www.book-cover-design.com
Editing: Judith Myers and Carl Minturn
Proofing: Joann Alsum and Cheryl Gort

Publisher's Cataloging-in-Publication (*Provided by Quality Books, Inc.*)

Palmer, David (David S.)
Parents' Guide to IQ Testing and Gifted Education: with a special section on bright kids with learning problems / David Palmer.
p. cm.
Includes bibliographical references and index.
LCCN 2005909269
ISBN 978-0-9771098-5-2

1. Gifted children-Education-United States.
2. Learning disabled children-Education-United States.
3. Parenting-United States.   I. Title.

LC3993.9.P35 2006   371.95'0973
QBI05-600169

To my family

CONTENTS

INTRODUCTION

What's In This Book?

IQ testing and selection for special programs is thought by some to be a mysterious and secretive domain understood only by the chosen few. It shouldn't be. To make meaningful decisions about your child's education you should have as much information as teachers, principals, school psychologists, or anyone else. In this book you'll find out how to recognize signs of giftedness and learning disabilities in your own child and learn how IQ tests and other criteria are used to select kids for special school programs. You don't necessarily need to read the chapters in order, or the book from cover to cover, to find what you're looking for. I'll outline what's ahead here so you can skip around a bit to find the exact information you want.

Chapter One: IQ tests can be used to make important decisions about the programs or services your child receives. For instance, IQ scores are often used when determining which students qualify for gifted education programs, or for resource programs designed to help kids with learning problems. Chapter One will help you understand what these tests measure and how to interpret the results so you can better work with those in the schools when making placement decisions for your child.

Chapter Two: Identifying gifted kids who need special support in school can be tricky. In fact, some kids with high IQs are better off in a regular school program. For this reason, IQ scores are usually only one of the criteria used when making placement decisions for gifted programs. Chapter Two reviews some of the other likely criteria and offers suggestions on how to work with the teacher to make sure that your child's learning needs are being met.

Chapter Three: If you're trying to decide whether a gifted education placement is right for your child, you'll need to understand what type of program your district is offering and how it differs from what your child is already getting. Chapter Three looks at common types of gifted programs and teaching techniques and offers specific questions for you to consider when thinking about your own child's needs. Alternatives to public school gifted programs are also considered.

Chapter Four: I've found that some parents are hesitant to ask questions about IQ testing and the gifted program selection process - maybe for fear of appearing pushy or overly concerned. Yet, parents need to have the same information as everyone else when it comes to making educational decisions for their children. In this chapter you'll get straight forward answers to the questions parents ask most.

Chapter Five: Your insights into your child's development are important, and the more knowledge you have, the better position you're in to partnership with others when selecting the best programs for your child. Chapter Five looks at some common traits of gifted kids and considers when early identification of giftedness may be needed.

Chapter Six: You don't necessarily have to have a high IQ to do well in life. Other traits like personal motivation, perseverance, and creativity may be just as - or more - important when it comes to happiness and success. In fact, there is little practical advantage, and maybe a real downside, to having an extremely high IQ. This chapter considers the idea of "optimal IQ" and looks at some of the potential negative aspects of giftedness.

Chapter Seven: There are lots of bright or gifted kids who struggle in school. Some of these may eventually be diagnosed with a learning disability and offered support. Yet, there are many others who could benefit from special school services but are never identified. Chapter Seven focuses on how to recognize learning problems in your own child and looks at different school programs that may help.

Chapter Eight: IQ testing has become commonplace in our schools. But how did this practice begin? The last three chapters of this book are for parents who want a deeper look at IQ testing and issues surrounding the concept of human intelligence. In Chapter Eight you'll get an overview of the early, sometimes bizarre, history of mental ability testing.

Chapter Nine: So what is intelligence? There really is no general agreement except to say that it's certainly more than what is measured on an IQ test. Chapter Nine looks at different perspectives on how to define intelligence and ends with a look at the theory of multiple intelligences - the idea that IQ tests measure only a very limited band of human abilities and may seriously underestimate our real potential.

Chapter Ten: Where do our abilities come from? How much of what we are is due to our genetics, and how much to our experiences? Chapter Ten looks at this question by considering studies of rats, twins, adoption, birth order, and family size.

A Note: I use the term "gifted" and "giftedness" throughout this book mostly to refer to the intellectually gifted - those that are likely to receive an unusually high score on an IQ test. Of course, there are lots of ways to be gifted, talented, exceptional, or extraordinary that can't be measured on such tests.

PART ONE

IQ Testing and Gifted Education

CHAPTER ONE

A Closer Look at IQ Tests
What They Measure and What the Scores Mean

Every day thousands of kids are being tested, sorted, and placed into special school programs based on a set of rules that many parents just don't understand. And why should they? Most parents don't have a background in testing and many aren't even aware that such programs exist. Their first exposure to these practices is usually when one of their own kids is in the system.

The key to helping your child get the most out of school is to understand how that system works. We'll start by looking at the basics of IQ testing - what these tests measure, how they are administered, and what the scores mean. IQ tests are often a major part of the selection criteria for school programs and these scores can be used to make important decisions about your child's education.

IQ and Intelligence

Some people think of the terms "IQ" and "intelligence" as interchangeable. But, that's not true. An IQ, or *intelligence quotient*, is just a number you get from taking an IQ test, while there is no real agreement on just how to define the term intelligence. The definition may change considerably from culture to culture, and even person to person, depending on who you ask or who you believe. So, if we can't agree on what constitutes intelligence, how can we measure it on an IQ test? We really can't.

What most do agree on is that IQ tests don't tap into all, or even most, areas of intelligence. In fact, critics argue that the skills that are measured are so narrow, so limited when compared to the broad range of human abilities and talents that are important for success and happiness in life, that IQ scores can give us a very restricted and misleading view of a person's true gifts and abilities. These tests are not designed to measure things like social skills, creativity, motivation, or self-esteem - all attributes which may be just as, or even more, important to your child's achievement and satisfaction than her IQ. So then, just what are IQ tests and what are they good for?

It is generally agreed that IQ tests do measure certain skills that are important to school learning, and that IQ scores are highly correlated to school achievement. In other words, children who do well on these tests tend to be those who get better grades in school. In that regard, IQ tests can probably best be viewed as predictors of school achievement.

What Do IQ Tests Measure?

While IQ tests measure certain skills that have been found to be strongly related to school achievement, each test publisher goes about measuring those skills in a different way, and may even measure quite different aspects of learning ability. The specific cognitive skills measured by each of these publishers may also change a bit every few years, as they periodically revise their tests to reflect current research and new ideas. To know exactly what learning skills (or cognitive domains) are measured by the most commonly used tests out there, you'd really need to pore over an up-to-date psychological assessment textbook. But for now, let's look at a few general areas that are commonly assessed on many IQ tests.

Remember, IQ tests are best seen as predictors of academic achievement. An IQ score only tells us how a certain child has performed on a certain test at a certain time, and says little about that child's true potential. Children can be gifted in many ways that are not measured on an IQ test.

Verbal Skills

The ability to understand and use words, to understand verbally presented information and answer comprehension questions, and the capacity to analyze and solve puzzles or problems in which verbal skills are involved.

Types of IQ test activities that may be used to measure these skills include:

- Defining words
- Answering questions which deal with an understanding of everyday life or with school learning
- Comparing and contrasting verbally presented concepts or explaining abstract ideas
- Solving word problems

Visual (or Nonverbal or Perceptual) Problem Solving

The ability to solve visually presented problems and puzzles, recognize visual patterns, and identify visual details.

Types of IQ test activities that may be used to measure these skills include:

- Putting puzzles together quickly and accurately
- Putting pictures in a certain order so they tell a story
- Assembling patterned blocks to match a model
- Choosing a picture from among several choices that completes a visual pattern or puzzle (Many internet IQ tests use this type of activity)

Memory

The ability to hold words, numbers, patterns, and symbols in the mind long enough to solve a problem or produce a response.

Types of IQ test activities that may be used to measure these skills include:

- Repeating back numbers, letters, or words spoken by the examiner
- Identifying specific details or events from a story that was read independently or read aloud by an examiner
- Placing colored beads or other objects on a table in a particular order after briefly viewing a model
- Remembering the sequence of objects or shapes briefly viewed in a picture or diagram.

Problem-Solving Speed

The ability to think and act quickly and to use available information to swiftly solve a problem.

Types of IQ test activities that may be used to measure these skills include:

- Copying symbols in a precise order within a certain time frame (The faster you go, the more points you get)

- Deciding whether two near-identical symbols are alike or different, within a certain time frame (Again, the faster you go, the more points you get)

Take a look at some of the skills measured on IQ tests and you can see why kids with higher IQ scores generally do better in school. Someone who has a good vocabulary and strong verbal skills should be able to apply those skills to lots of school-related tasks - like reading, understanding a social studies text book, or solving math word problems on a test. In the same way, a child who shows advanced visual problem-solving ability while putting together puzzles or figuring out visual patterns would likely be good at seeing patterns or relationships in areas such as math and science. And, of course, there's an obvious connection between memory and speed of problem solving and being able to perform well at school.

Two Types of Tests

There are two basic types of IQ tests - group tests and individually administered tests. Although both attempt to measure skills involved in school learning, there are some important differences in both format and content.

Group Tests

Group tests are meant to be given to a large group of children at one time. They are developed to be user friendly, and can be given by teachers or others not specifically trained in IQ test administration.

When administering a group test, the teacher passes out booklets to his students, makes sure everyone understands how to correctly mark the answers to the questions, and then, reading from a script, gives directions on how to complete each section.

Depending on the type of test item and the age of the children, the teacher may read the instructions or questions out loud or the children may be asked to work independently. The teacher will also typically review sample problems in each section to be sure that everyone understands what they are to do before beginning.

Many group tests are completed in an hour or two, and can be administered in one or two sessions. Since these tests are standardized, the teacher cannot give any extra help to individual students who may need extra assistance. Rather, students may be given instructions like, "Do your best," or, "Choose the best answer and move on to the next problem" if they become stuck or frustrated.

Because group tests are designed to be administered quickly and measure only a limited set of cognitive skills, they are not considered to be as reliable or as accurate as individually administered tests. Due to these limitations, group tests are often thought of as screening assessments and many (perhaps most) districts use them primarily to select students for further testing with an individually administered IQ test.

Individually Administered Tests

Individually administered tests are given in a one-on-one setting. Some common versions of these tests for school-age kids are the Wechsler Intelligence Scale for Children (or WISC - pronounced "Wisk"), the Stanford-Binet Intelligence Scale, and the Kaufman Assessment Battery for Children.

"What about internet IQ tests - the kind you can take online? Are those *real* tests, and can you believe the results?" If you've got an internet connection, you can easily find a website where you can take a self-administered IQ test and, often for a fee or in exchange for allowing your email address to be put on a mailing list, get an "IQ" score. But how valid are the results? It's hard to say. Many online tests measure only limited aspects of intelligence and have not been as thoroughly researched and "standardized" (a long and expensive process that allows one person's test scores to be compared to another's) when compared to the traditional tests that professionals use. I've known many people who have taken an online test and scored in the "genius" range. So, even if the results aren't always perfectly accurate, online tests may be a great way to get a quick ego boost.

In contrast to group IQ tests, individually administered IQ tests:

- May take longer to administer and score
- Must be given only by a qualified examiner such as a school psychologist or a clinical psychologist
- Measure a wider range of skills - typically including more specific aspects of verbal and nonverbal reasoning, tasks involving motor skills, and tasks involving speed of problem solving

Because they measure a broader range of abilities and are administered by trained examiners, individually administered IQ tests are considered to be more reliable than group tests. For this reason, many districts base educational decisions - like placement in a gifted education program or eligibility for special education services - on these scores. We'll focus on the individually administered IQ test in the rest of this chapter.

What's It Like to Take an Individually Administered IQ Test?

IQ tests are standardized tests. They have been developed so that one child's score can be easily compared to another's. But for this comparison to be valid examiners must be sure to give the test in a standard way - they must use the same testing procedures for each child. For example, the same directions must be given, the same time limits must apply, and the same scoring criteria must be used. It wouldn't make sense to give one child extra time to complete a test item, or to give him hints or added encouragement, and then compare that child's score with another's who wasn't given such advantages.

While specific directions and standard administration procedures will differ a bit from test to test, there is a common set of general guidelines, a familiar flow, to all individually administered IQ tests.

- Before the examiner starts testing, he will spend some time building rapport - making small talk and checking to be sure that the child is comfortable and does not appear ill or overly anxious. This is an important part of the standardized test procedure and experienced examiners should be experts at making children feel at ease.

- Individually administered IQ tests are made up of several smaller *subtests*. Children in certain age groups are generally given the same subtests in the same order. The examiner will determine the sequence of subtests to give a child by determining his age and maybe by giving him a brief placement or *routing* test.

- Items on each subtest are presented in order of increasing difficulty. The examiner will determine by the child's age, or through the routing test, the item to begin with on each subtest - this is often called the *starting point*. Subtests are designed so that children start with items that they can pass easily, to give them a feeling of success.

- The examiner will be sure that the child understands what he is to do on each subtest before beginning. Most subtests require the examiner to give sample items so that the child has an opportunity to practice whatever the task requires before moving on to the actual test items. These sample items are generally not scored.

- The examiner will move through the subtests in the sequence dictated by the test manual for the child's age level or ability level. While administering the test, the examiner will be scoring the child's responses. Examiners are trained to do this in such a way as not to call attention to the scoring procedure - so as not to give the child any feedback regarding whether their responses are correct or not.

- The examiner will stop testing on most subtests when the child has made a certain number of errors. The subtests are designed this way so that children do not become frustrated or discouraged by being given test items that would be too difficult for their age or ability level. The test item where the examiner stops is usually called the *ceiling item* or *stopping point*.

- Some of the subtests - usually those that involve having the child do something like put puzzles together or write things down rather than just answer questions - may be timed and scored based on the quickness of the response. The examiner will use a stopwatch or maybe a wristwatch to do this, being careful to be as unobtrusive as possible so that the child doesn't feel pressured or distracted. In my experience, most children do not even realize they are being timed.

- The examiner will do his best to continue to make the child feel comfortable throughout the IQ test, putting him at ease by making informal conversation or encouraging comments.

- Most individually administered IQ tests take about an hour and a half to administer. When the test is over, the examiner will praise the child for his effort and participation, continuing to make him feel at ease and assured.

And that's it. Most kids actually seem to enjoy being tested. They probably like the individual attention they get, and the chance to get out of class for a while.

Three Types of IQ Scores

The purpose of giving an IQ test in the schools is to get a score, or set of scores, that can be used to predict a child's learning ability and make educational placement decisions. Let's take a look at the three different types of scores that you'll need to know about when interpreting IQ tests.

Subtest Scores

As you've read, individually administered IQ tests are made up of several smaller tests called *subtests*. Each of these subtests involves a different type of activity and measures a particular area of ability. For example, a subtest that measures attention and memory skills may require the child to listen to and repeat back numbers spoken by the examiner. Another subtest measuring visual problem solving skills might involve the child putting blocks together to match a design shown in a picture. Usually around ten or so of these individual subtests are administered during an IQ test, with each taking about ten minutes to give.

Psychologists often don't report subtest scores to parents because they are not as reliable as other IQ scores, which are obtained by combining subtest scores. It's like averaging grades. Your child might get one poor grade on a spelling test but this doesn't necessarily mean he's a bad speller. If you average several of his spelling grades, however, you get a better picture of his true spelling abilities.

Subscale Scores

A *subscale* score gives you information about a child's performance in a certain skill area - or *cognitive domain*. To arrive at subscale scores (sometimes called process scores, factor index scores, composite scores, or some other such name) two or more subtest scores are combined, based on what is being measured. For example, if three of ten subtests given during an IQ test deal largely with short-term memory skills, then the scores from these subtests may be combined into a "Short-Term Memory Subscale" score. Other subtests might be grouped into subscales that measure areas like verbal reasoning skills, visual reasoning skills, or speed of problem solving. Most individually administered IQ tests are designed to measure around five to seven subscales areas.

"School Psychologists and Clinical Psychologists? What's the difference?" A clinical psychologist typically practices in non-educational areas with private clients, or through agencies not associated with a school district. Clinical psychologists are licensed to provide therapy and typically have some training in the administration of IQ tests - but they may not regularly administer them as part of their regular routine. A school psychologist, also called an educational psychologist, is specifically credentialed to work in the public school setting, and may also be licensed (by passing a state exam and meeting other requirements) to provide private educational therapy and testing. School psychologists often have the most experience with IQ testing as this tends to be a regular part of their job responsibilities. Some states also allow licensed psychometrists to administer IQ tests. A psychometrist is basically an expert in testing, but is not trained to provide therapy or counseling.

Subscale scores can tell you a lot about your child's relative strengths and weaknesses. While some students do about equally well on all subscale areas, many show some pretty large differences. A child with a strong verbal reasoning subscale score and a relatively low visual (perceptual) reasoning subscale score, for instance, may learn more efficiently through lectures or just sitting down with a book, rather than through diagrams, charts, or mentally picturing an idea. A child with a relatively low score on a subscale dealing with memory may need more repetition before basic skills are mastered. A child with a relatively low score on a subscale involving processing speed (the ability to think and act quickly) may be a perfectionist who works more slowly than others because of a tendency to check her work for accuracy before moving on.

Remember that each IQ test is organized differently, and that subscale results may be interpreted differently from test to test. Ask your child's examiner to help you review and interpret the subscale scores provided on the particular test used for your child. And remember to combine your own observations and instincts with any test scores you're reviewing when considering your child's learning needs.

Full Scale Score

The *full scale* (or composite) score is what most people probably think of when they hear the term "IQ." Unlike subscale scores, which reflect a child's performance in particular skill areas, the full-scale score reflects the child's overall performance - taking into account the diverse mix of mental abilities sampled on all the subtests. It is often the full-scale IQ score that is used to make educational placement decisions regarding entrance into a gifted education program or eligibility for special education services.

While the full scale IQ may give you a good overall sense of how your child did on the test, subscale scores are more useful for understanding your child's pattern of abilities.

Understanding IQ Scores

Once an IQ test has been administered, the examiner adds up the points the child earned on each of the subtests. He then converts these points into a *standard score* by comparing the child's performance to others in the same age category. This can be done manually by using tables in a testing manual, or with the help of a software program provided by the test publisher. The subscale and the full-scale IQ standard scores are obtained in a similar way.

A standard score is a number that can be used to compare the performance of one person to another. Standard scores are designed to have a *mean* and a *standard deviation*. The mean is the average score on the test while the standard deviation deals with how scores are distributed around the mean. I won't go into these statistical concepts here, but simply say that most IQ test publishers design their tests so that the mean, the average score, is set at 100 and the standard deviation is set at 15. Often, both full-scale scores and subscale scores are designed like this. These are the types of scores we'll be considering from here on out.

Descriptions

Someone receiving an IQ score of 100 has scored right at the mean - the average. Half the people in the age group she is being compared to have scored higher and half have scored lower. Of course, IQ scores are not usually exactly 100. How well someone did on an IQ test is usually determined by how far above or below the average their score falls. So how about a score of 93, how does that compare to the average? Or a score of 117, what does that mean?

Many examiners will help parents interpret their child's IQ scores by using descriptive terms for different score ranges. These terms are provided by the test publisher in the manual provided with the test.

To avoid showing our ignorance, many of us tend to smile and nod knowingly when listening to an "expert" explain something we don't quite understand. But when reviewing your child's test scores, don't hesitate to ask questions. Test publishers may use different terms, theories, and statistics when describing subscale scores and test performance. Part of the examiner's job is to explain the results of a particular IQ test in simple, everyday terms. If you don't understand something, ask the examiner to explain it to you again, in clearer terms. You might say something like "Tell me exactly what that means," or "Could you go over that again? I didn't quite get it." It's better to spend a few minutes asking questions when you've got the chance than to end up with lots of question marks floating around in your head on your ride home.

Here's an example of some commonly used descriptive terms associated with IQ scores:

IQ Score	Descriptive Term	% of Population
130 and above	Very superior or gifted	2.2 percent
120 to 129	Superior	6.7 percent
110 to 119	High average	16.1 percent
90 to 109	Average	50 percent
80 to 89	Low average	16.1 percent
70 to 79	Borderline Delayed	6.7 percent
69 and below	Delayed	2.2 percent

Looking at this table, you can see that half of all people taking an IQ test score between 90 and 109. And as you get further away from average, in either direction, the fewer people there are in those score categories. Only about two percent of those taking an IQ test score in the gifted range

By using descriptive terms, you should be able to get a good sense of what your child's score means. But as you can see, the score ranges are pretty broad. And keep in mind that different test publishers, researchers, and advocates may use different terms, or different score breakdowns, when describing test performance. For example, instead of calling scores between 90 and 109 average, some may say that scores between 85 and 114 are in the average range. Also, while our table calls the score range between 120 and 129 "superior," others may refer to these scores as being in the "mildly gifted" or "very bright" range. You get the idea. The words used are just that - words. Don't read too much into the terms, and keep in mind that there are no universally accepted definitions when it comes to describing IQ levels.

Levels of Giftedness

IQ scores above 130 can also be categorized into different levels of giftedness.

Here's one set of terms commonly used to describe these categories:

- 130 to 144   Moderately Gifted
- 145 to 159   Highly Gifted
- 160 to 179   Exceptionally Gifted
- 180 and above   Profoundly Gifted

Estimates differ when it comes to the number of children scoring in the extremes of the gifted range. This is partly because standard scores on most traditional IQ test scores only go up to around 160, so higher IQ scores sometimes have to be estimated through a combination of different assessment instruments, some of which may not be as current or well researched as the more traditional tests.

One estimate is that:

- Fewer than 1 out of 1000 have an IQ of 145
- Fewer than 1 out of 10,000 have an IQ of 160
- Fewer than 1 out of 100,000 have an IQ of 180

Standard Scores and Percentiles

Another way to interpret standard scores involves the use of percentile ranks. A percentile rank (or percentile or percentile score) indicates the percentage of other children in the same age category that the test taker scored as well as, or better than.

- For example, if a child earned a percentile rank of 27 on an IQ test, that means that she did as well as, or better than, 27 percent of the children she is being compared to.
- If a child earned a percentile rank of 95 on an IQ test, that means that she did as well as, or better than, 95 percent of the children she is being compared to.

In the same way, every possible standard score is associated with a specific percentile rank. For instance, a standard score of 90 is associated with a percentile rank of 25, a standard score of 100 is associated with a percentile rank of 50, a standard score of 110 is associated with a percentile rank of 75, and so on.

The examiner should tell you your child's percentile scores when reviewing the test results. You can also look them up yourself, once you know your child's standard score, by using a *Standard Score to Percentile Conversion Table* such as the one provided on the next page.

Standard Scores and Percentile Ranks

Standard Score	%ile Rank	Standard Score	%ile Rank
133	99	99	47
132	98	98	45
131	98	97	42
130	98	96	39
129	97	95	37
128	97	94	34
127	96	93	32
126	96	92	30
125	95	91	27
124	95	90	25
123	94	89	23
122	93	88	21
121	92	87	19
120	91	86	18
119	90	85	16
118	88	84	14
117	87	83	13
116	86	82	12
115	84	81	10
114	82	80	9
113	81	79	8
112	79	78	7
111	77	77	6
110	75	76	5
109	73	75	5
108	70	74	4
107	68	73	4
106	65	72	3
105	63	71	3
104	61	70	2
103	58	69	2
102	55	68	2
101	53	67	1
100	50	66	1

Note: This table is valid for all IQ scores where the mean is set at 100 and the standard deviation is 15. Most tests are organized this way. If you are reviewing a test that is organized differently (such as an older version of the Stanford-Binet Intelligence Scale where the standard deviation is set at 16) the examiner will use a different table to convert standard scores to percentiles.

Percentile Ranks and Percentages.
What's the Difference?

A lot of people confuse *percentile ranks* with *percentages* when trying to interpret IQ scores. Don't let this happen to you.

Here's the difference:

- A percentile rank indicates the percentage of others that the test taker scored as well as, or better than.

- A percentage tells us how many answers out of 100 are correct.

Researchers have found that over the past several decades performance on IQ tests has improved steadily. In fact, on average, IQ scores in the U.S. and many other countries appear to have gone up by about three points every decade. Why? No one knows for sure. Strange as it seems, it continues to happen. Because of this curious phenomenon children who take the most recent revisions of an IQ test tend to score a few points lower than those who take an older version. This is because their test performance is compared to the more recent and "smarter" group of people that the test has been normed on.

For instance, if you have a test with 100 questions, and you get 65 of them right, then you got 65 percent of the questions correct.

Of course, most tests don't have exactly 100 questions, so figuring out the percentage of correct responses isn't always that straightforward. But you can get a percentage correct on any test with any number of questions simply by dividing the number correct by the number of items on the test, and then moving the decimal over a couple of spaces to the right.

- For example, if someone gets 32 answers right on a test with 40 questions, he received 80 percent correct. Try it. Get out a calculator and divide 32 by 40. You'll get 0.8. Now move the decimal over a couple of spaces to the right and you'll get 80. 80 percent correct.

In this way, teachers and others can convert all test scores to percentages, which makes it easy to assign grades. It's a common practice. Anyone who's been to school is familiar with this grade formula for converting percentages into letter grades:

- Percentage scores between 90 and 100 result in a grade of A
- Percentage scores between 80 and 89 result in a grade of B
- Percentage scores between 70 and 79 result in a grade of C
- Percentage scores between 60 and 69 result in a grade of D
- Percentage scores below 59 result in a grade of F.

And this is where the confusion comes in. This grading formula is so pervasive that we have become used to thinking in terms of percentages whenever we hear the root word "percent." Parents can be quite distressed to learn that their child earned a percentile rank of 68 on an IQ test, if they're thinking in terms of percentages. On a regular test, a percentage score of 68 would only earn you a letter grade of "D."

On the other hand, a *percentile rank* of 68 is pretty good. In fact, it's above average since it means that the test taker did as well as or better than 68 percent of those taking the same test. Remember that a percentile rank of 50 is exactly average and is associated with the exact average standard score of 100 on an IQ test. A percentile ranking of 68 on an IQ test is above average and associated with a standard score of 107.

Age Equivalent Scores

Age equivalent scores (sometimes called test age equivalents or something similar) are the average scores, expressed in years and months, obtained by various age groups of children.

Age-equivalent scores are calculated by noting the average number of items a certain age group gets correct on a test. Any other test taker that gets the same number correct is given that age-equivalent score. For instance, if it was found that the average number of items answered correctly by children who were 10 years, 7 months of age on a particular IQ subtest was 17 out of a possible 20, then anyone getting 17 items correct on that subtest can be said to have an age equivalent score of 10-7.

While age-equivalent scores can give parents a general sense of how their child has performed, these scores are often not reported since they can be misleading and may give the impression that a test taker's performance is really much higher or lower than it actually is.

CHAPTER ONE

A Closer Look at IQ Tests

Quick Points

- While IQ tests don't measure all aspects of intelligence, they do measure certain skills that are associated with school learning. For this reason, IQ tests might best be thought of as predictors of school achievement.

- The specific kinds of learning skills measured by different IQ tests vary from one test publisher to the next. A few general areas that are measured on many IQ tests include:

  > Verbal Skills
  > Visual Problem-Solving Skills
  > Memory
  > Problem-Solving Speed

- The two general types of IQ tests used in the schools are the group test and the individually administered test. While both are designed to measure certain cognitive traits that are important for school learning, individually administered tests typically measure a wider range of skills and are usually considered to be more reliable.

- Individually administered IQ tests are given by a trained examiner such as a clinical or educational psychologist, and take an hour or two to administer. Examiners use the same standard testing procedures with every child, which includes establishing rapport and trying to make the child feel at ease and successful.

- IQ tests yield three types of scores: subtest scores, subscale scores, and the full scale (or composite) score.

➤ A subtest score reflects the child's performance on one of the individual activities within an IQ test that measures a particular skill or ability.

➤ A subscale score is obtained when two or more sub-tests are combined to reflect the child's performance in a general area, like memory or verbal skills.

➤ The full scale score is what most people think of when they hear the term "IQ," and reflects the child's over-all performance on the test.

• The scores derived from IQ testing are called standard scores. Standard scores are designed so that one person's test score can be easily compared to another's.

• Two common ways of interpreting standard scores are by using descriptive terms, like "average" or "high average," or by looking at the percentile rank associated with the score. A percentile rank tells the percentage of those that the test taker scored as well as, or better than, on a particular test. For example, if a child receives a percentile rank of 85 on a test, that means that she scored as well as, or bet-ter than, 85 percent of those in the age group that she is being compared to.

CHAPTER TWO

Identifying Gifted Students
Who Gets Tested and Why

IQ testing isn't a regular part of most kids' school experience. In fact, a very small percentage of students are ever offered an individually administered IQ test. Why? It's expensive, time consuming, and not necessary for most children. Typical students can thrive in a typical classroom with a teacher who is trained to meet the average range of abilities found there.

An individual IQ test is usually only given when it appears that a child is out of sync with the typical learner. Children who are intellectually gifted may be in this group. These children might appear bored or frustrated by the general education curriculum. Their academic skills may be well beyond their years and their overwhelming curiosity or diversity of interests can make it difficult for a general education teacher to provide them with learning opportunities they require. These students may have social differences too - appearing not to "connect" with other children, or preferring the company of adults to children.

But how should schools go about identifying who to test and who needs gifted program services in order to flourish? Not all bright children are gifted, and not all gifted children are so different from their peers that they need special support. For this reason, nearly all districts have developed a systematic way to screen students for such programs.

There is no federal law that mandates how school districts identify gifted children, and there is no universal agreement as to what constitutes intelligence or "giftedness." Still, many districts use an individually administered IQ test as at least part of their screening process - and those that do often use the IQ score as the primary condition of placement. However flawed or controversial these tests may be, they are arguably the best tool we have to find kids who learn differently.

IQ tests measure such things as problem solving skills, memory, and the ability to understand and use language - some of the same skills that are used in the classroom. It follows, then, that those who score unusually well on these tests will likely be unusual learners who need a program that is different than that provided in the most classrooms.

How Are Gifted Students Identified?

There are many ways to be gifted. And some school districts, typically the larger ones, will have special programs for students talented in areas not measured on IQ tests. Magnet schools for those gifted in the arts, for example, with entrance based on teacher recommendations, judged performances, or a portfolio review. And virtually all school districts will have programs for the physically gifted - varsity level sports teams, where students with exceptional talent in a particular sport compete against each other to be placed on a team with other students of similar ability.

Identifying exceptional children for these programs is sometimes a difficult task. There is always some subjectivity in deciding who makes varsity, for example, or which dancer, painter, or musician is talented enough to be accepted into an arts magnet program. Identifying children who will benefit from a program for the intellectually gifted can also be difficult. One obstacle involves trying to distinguish bright, high-achieving students who may be best served in a traditional classroom from those who have such advanced abilities, and learn so differently, that they need a different kind of school experience to succeed.

This distinction would be easy if all gifted children acted the same. But, of course, they don't. In fact, they are often more different from one another than they are from many of their average-ability peers.

- Some are highly excitable and outgoing, while others are quiet and introspective
- Some excel academically, while others are underachievers
- Some appear extremely focused in the classroom, while others appear highly inattentive
- Some are model students, never getting into any trouble at school, while others always seem to test the rules

Using a limited approach to identification, such as teacher recommendation or a review of grades or achievement test scores, just won't work. High-achieving children may be identified this way, but not the intellectually gifted. For this reason, most districts use a multifaceted approach to identification, basing the selection of children on a variety of screening methods. Each district will have a specific person or team who determines what criteria to use. Some may rate children on a point scale in several areas, including how they score on an individual IQ test, and then offer gifted program services to those receiving a certain number of points. Others use multiple screening methods largely to select children for an individual IQ test and then use the score on that test as the final criterion on which selection is made.

You've read about the basics of Individual IQ testing in Chapter One and in Chapter Four I'll answer many of the specific questions that parents often ask about IQ tests and gifted education. In the rest of this chapter, we'll look at other selection criteria that districts commonly use when selecting for gifted programs.

Teacher or Parent Nominations

Often the screening process starts when a teacher nominates a student for a gifted program. Districts, or individual schools, may have a set procedure and time frame for such nominations. For example, teachers may be asked to submit names at the end of the first semester. Other districts may be more informal, allowing teachers to submit names of students at any time of the year. Some districts let teachers use their own judgment when nominating students, while others ask that they select only those who match a predetermined list of characteristics.

Districts may also ask parents to nominate their own children to be evaluated for the district's gifted program. Even districts that do not actively solicit parents' nominations will often screen a child if a parent requests that they do so.

Rating Scales

Teachers, and sometimes parents, may be asked to fill out checklists or rating scales regarding their observations of the child. This step helps adults to look more objectively at the child's behaviors and allows program evaluators the chance to compare the child's profile with others who are being screened. The rater will be asked to compare the child to a list of characteristics that are typically associated with gifted students. On some scales, the rater is simply asked to indicate whether the child shows a particular trait or not. On others, they are asked to assign points to the child, based on how strongly they agree that he matches the set of characteristics being described.

Below are some common traits that may be included on a rating scale for giftedness.

- ➘ Masters academic skills and concepts quickly and easily

- ➘ Demonstrates an overwhelming curiosity

- ➘ Has an advanced vocabulary

- ➘ Has an excellent memory

- ➘ Prefers to socialize with older peers or adults

- ➘ Has many interests or hobbies

- ➘ Shows reading and/or math skills that are well above age or grade

- ➘ Seems to truly enjoy the process of learning and seeks out new learning experiences independently

- ➘ Demonstrates a focused interest in a specific or unusual area of study

- ➘ Is highly sensitive and/or shows a strong sense of compassion for others

- ➘ Good at problem solving or reasoning

- ➘ Has an advanced sense of humor

- ➘ Is able to maintain interest and focus for long periods of time

Some districts also use rating scales to assess whether a child would be a good candidate for the particular type of gifted education program being offered. For example, if the district's program involves independent study, the scale would have questions about the child's ability to be self-directed and self-motivated. If the district's program is based on group or cooperative learning, then the scale would have a few questions regarding the child's ability to work cooperatively as part of a team.

Formal Observation

Once a child has been nominated by a teacher or a parent, someone from the school or district may do a formal observation in the classroom as a way to gather further information and get an objective second opinion regarding the recommendation. The observer, who may be a school psychologist, principal, learning specialist, or district representative associated with the gifted program, may use a structured observation form or checklist to guide their observation. The observer may also interact with the child in the classroom to get a better sense of how he relates and learns.

Input From Past Teachers

Previous teachers may be interviewed or asked to complete a rating scale, to get their perspective on the child's learning needs. Sometimes the child's current teacher, past teachers, and other district representatives such as the school principal, the resource specialist, and the school psychologist will meet together to come up with a group recommendation. These types of group meetings, often called a *Student Study Team* meeting or something similar, are also used by many schools when discussing students who need special academic intervention, or who may need special education support.

A Review of Past Grades or Test Scores

The child's current and past grades, scores on state achievement tests, and any other class or school-wide achievement testing will be reviewed. The district may require that a student's grades and test scores meet a certain standard for the screening process to continue. Many districts place a great deal of weight on students' grades and test scores, reasoning that, even if children measure in the gifted range on an IQ test, they may not possess the motivation, independence, or other characteristics needed to do well in a gifted program where these traits are often critical.

Parent Interest

At some point in the screening process a district representative will ask parents if they are interested in having their child participate in the program. Some parents will not be interested, for a variety of reasons. For example, if the placement involves a move to a different campus or a different classroom, away from the child's friends, the parents may want to keep their child where he is for social purposes. And sometimes parents may simply not agree with the "philosophy" of gifted education - seeing it as elitist or a form of segregation.

Of course, no matter what the district's recommendation, the final decision regarding placement is yours to make. Districts generally won't push a parent into placing a child in a gifted education program.

Student Interest and Attitudes

A child who is being considered for a gifted program may be interviewed or asked to complete an interest survey. For example, if the program involves independent research and long-term independent projects, the district may want to see if the child expresses a desire to move ahead of the class, explore specialized topics on his own, and work independently.

Placement Trials

Students may be placed on a trial basis in a classroom or group where the teacher uses the same type of learning strategies that are used by the school's gifted program teachers. The purpose is to identify students who may thrive in the specific type of program the district offers. In these placement trials students may be encouraged to work more independently, design their own learning goals, or work cooperatively with others on a long-term project.

Placement trials may be carried out by the child's own teacher who presents a lesson, or several lessons over time, using the alternative gifted program strategies within his or her own classroom. Or these trials may involve a specialist, such as the coordinator of gifted education or a gifted education teacher, who comes in to present lessons to a whole classroom of students or to a selected group of children who are being screened.

Portfolio Review

Some districts encourage the use of portfolios in the assessment of student performance. A portfolio is really just a systematic collection of a student's work. For example, a writing portfolio is a collection of a child's writing over the course of a certain time period, such as a semester or a year. Portfolio work samples are often sequenced from earliest to latest examples to allow the student, as well as teachers and parents, to evaluate progress and development over time. Many educators believe that the use of portfolios is a more meaningful way of evaluating a student's progress than simply giving tests and issuing report cards.

Part of the process of screening for a gifted education program may include a review of the student's work samples collected over time in such portfolios. The student's work may be evaluated against the work of others for such characteristics as quality, depth, effort, and ability.

Group IQ tests

Districts will often screen large groups of children - sometimes entire grades - with a group IQ test at a predetermined time each year. For example, every October all second graders in a district will be administered a group IQ test by their teachers. Many gifted kids don't shine in school - their abilities may be masked by boredom, frustration, disorganization, or other common traits of giftedness. Group tests are often used as an objective way to identify children for further screening who may have been overlooked.

Group tests can be administered as early as kindergarten, yet many districts will only begin using them in second or third grade, in part because programs for gifted learners often don't begin until this time. Another reason for waiting to administer these tests is that older children's scores tend to be more reliable. Taking a group test requires certain skills - such as concentration, focus, and the ability to independently follow through on whole-class directions - which improve with developmental maturity.

Group test scores are not considered to be as reliable as individually administered IQ test scores. For this reason, a child's performance on a group test is usually not the main factor on which a gifted program placement is made. More likely, a child's score on these tests will be used in conjunction with other criteria when determining eligibility. Or the group test score will be used to determine whether a child is a good candidate to be tested with an individually administered IQ test.

Your Child and the Screening Process

Using the strategies outlined in this chapter, schools should be able to identify most students who would benefit from a gifted education placement, so you may not need to do anything to ensure that your child is being fairly evaluated by "the system."

Yet, there may be times when you feel that the school is missing something about your child, and you'd like to be sure that he or she is being given the same consideration and opportunities as others.

Maybe you've heard from other parents that their children are being screened for the district's program, and you're thinking, "What about my kid? I know she's just as smart!" Or you find out that your child was being considered but did not "make the cut" for some reason. While you don't want to be perceived as overly protective or pushy, you also want to make sure that those making the decisions have all the information they need to truly understand your child.

Some gifted children are not identified because their potential is masked by personality traits - such as shyness, low frustration tolerance, or an overly easy-going nature. Giftedness may also be hidden by a child's social and language background, or by a specific learning disability (yes, kids can be both gifted and learning disabled; Chapter Seven looks at this topic). If you believe this is true in your child's case, you may want to talk with the teacher and share your thoughts.

Parents and teachers are a child's most important allies and they need to keep each other informed and up to date. Each sees the child from a different perspective and each has a particular insight into a child's learning needs. As a parent, you've watched your child's development since birth. You've seen him at home, at play, with friends, and with family. You're in a good position to truly understand his specific interests, temperament, unique gifts, strengths, and limitations. The teacher, on the other hand, has had an opportunity to evaluate your child's learning style, academic skills, and social and cognitive development in comparison to a large number of other children of the same age. It doesn't take long for most experienced teachers to develop an intuitive sense of their students' strengths and needs - to evaluate how quickly they learn, the type of instruction they respond to best, and their attitudes toward school. The teacher may also help you to better understand the district's gifted education program and how it is different than what your child is already receiving.

Together, you should be able to get a more complete, objective view than either of you had on your own. Maybe you'll come to realize that your child would be better off in a general education program since his learning style would not mesh with the type of curriculum being used in the district's gifted program. On the other hand, the teacher may consider taking a second look at your child in light of the extra information you have given her.

If you've already talked with the teacher and you still feel that your child's needs are not being met, then consider following up on your request with an administrator. Find out through conversations with other parents, or by a phone call to the district office, who is in charge of the gifted program selection process at your child's school. Then write a politely worded letter stating your concerns. Also consider sending a copy to the district's coordinator of gifted education, the school principal, and the teacher.

Now all you need to do is allow those involved to respond and let the district's screening process take over. Districts generally want to work with parents and will follow up on most reasonable requests.

Working Together

A key to developing a productive relationship with those at your child's school is to make a commitment to work collaboratively and to stay positive. Below are some general tips for developing a mutually supportive relationship with your child's teachers. These tips assume that the teacher is a competent and caring person (most teachers are) who has good professional judgment and truly knows how to teach (most teachers do).

View the Teacher as a Partner, a Collaborator, and a Co-Advocate for Your Child

See the teacher as another person on your child's team who is on your side and wants the very best for your child.

Stay Involved

This applies not just when there is a concern or a problem, but when things are going well. Communicate with the teacher on a regular basis. Stay in tune with how your child is doing at school. You might even volunteer in your child's classroom if you have the time. If not, find other ways to support the teacher and the school - show up to Back To School Night and parent conferences, donate supplies, volunteer to help at the school carnival, work with the PTA.

Keep an Open Mind and Support the Teacher's Classroom Procedures

Teachers have different teaching styles. For example, some are quite strict, some more relaxed when it comes to things like discipline and homework. What works for one teacher may not for another. I remember when one of my own children had a teacher who was very focused on building independence and personal responsibility. The first few weeks, my impulse was to step in and "save" him when something was late, or not written down in his organizer. However, I followed this teacher's plan and let him be solely responsible for getting assignments done, and for taking the consequences when they weren't. As a result, he developed excellent organization and homework habits that carried through to other grades.

When You Have a Concern

Examine Your Motives

You are your child's primary advocate, and you should speak up when it comes to making sure that her needs are being met at school. But it doesn't hurt to do a little self-reflection first, to make sure you're speaking up for the right reasons. For example, if your concern is about your child being accepted into a gifted program, check that your primary motivation is not your own need for your child to be labeled as gifted because you believe this will raise your own esteem or give you bragging rights with other parents.

Get informed

It's possible that your concern can be resolved by just understanding the school or class policies better. If your concern is about how children are identified for the district's gifted education program, then getting a written copy of the selection criteria or district policy may answer many of your questions. If the concern is about a classroom procedure, regarding homework or discipline for example, then clarifying these procedures with the teacher may put you at ease.

Speak to the Teacher Directly

When you have a question or an issue you'd like to address, take it to the teacher directly. Schedule an appointment and talk to her privately. A sure way to damage your relationship with your child's teacher (and probably with others at the school, as well) is to go to the principal or other administrator with a concern before giving the teacher a chance to resolve it. Again, think of the teacher as a partner, a collaborator, and a co-advocate for your child. If you've gone to her first, and feel you are not being heard, then consider involving administrators.

Stay positive and collaborative

Let the teacher know your concerns politely and directly.   Use the kind of effective communication skills that are useful in any situation - make good eye contact and actively listen to and try to understand the other person's point of view. Most importantly, stay focused on working together as a team to come up with ideas and solutions that will work for your child.

CHAPTER TWO

Identifying Gifted Students

Quick Points

- Only a small percentage of children in public schools are ever offered an individually administered IQ test.

- IQ tests in the schools are primarily used to identify students who learn differently and who may need special support services.

- Most schools use multiple screening criteria, often including an IQ test score, to determine who qualifies for a gifted program.

- Some districts use multiple screening criteria largely to determine which children will be offered an individually administered IQ test, and then base the placement decision primarily on that score.

- In addition to the use of an individually administered IQ test, some of the other criteria that districts use to determine eligibility for a gifted education program include:

  - ➥ Teacher or parent referrals

  - ➥ A review of checklist or rating scale results

  - ➥ Formal observation by a district representative or specialist

  - ➥ Input from past teachers

  - ➥ A review of past and current grades and test scores

  - ➥ Parent interest

  - ➥ Student interest and attitude

➤ Evaluation of how the student responds to a placement trial

➤ A review of a student's portfolio

➤ Scores obtained on a group IQ test

• Parents and teachers are a child's best advocates and, by working together, are in an ideal position to identify a child's unique learning needs.

CHAPTER THREE

What is Gifted Education?

And is it Right for My Child?

Gifted education can take many different forms, determined by the philosophy of the school and even the funds available from the district. And whether the program you're considering is right for your child is a personal decision, one you'll have to make. But first you'll need information - about what the district is offering, how it differs from what your child is already getting, and whether the program fits his or her needs.

Below, we'll consider the purpose for gifted programs and go over some questions you might ask yourself when considering your options. Later, I'll review some of the more common forms that gifted education takes, and go over some alternatives to placement.

Gifted Programs - Are They Really Necessary?

It's part of human nature to want to learn, to be in that place where we feel we are growing intellectually, spiritually, and creatively. We want to feel challenged, to move beyond where we are and toward our innate potential, to test our limits. Abraham Maslow, the well-known humanistic psychologist, called this the tendency toward self-actualization, and viewed it as a central human drive.

Children need to feel challenged too. In order to stay engaged, interested, and excited about learning they need the opportunity to explore, create, grow, and go off in their own directions. Most children can find these opportunities in a general education classroom with a teacher who is skilled at challenging and motivating her students. But some children are so different, so off the curve when it comes to how they learn, that they need more. For this kind of child, the typical school experience can become suffocating.

Many advocates of gifted education draw an analogy between children who are intellectually gifted and those whose gifts are in other areas, such as music or athletics. You wouldn't put a violin prodigy who was playing Bach concertos in with a group of children who were just starting to master their instruments and expect her to learn much. You wouldn't coach a star basketball player, golfer, or swimmer the same way you'd coach a beginner. Those whose skills and abilities are already advanced in a certain area need the opportunity to learn alongside others with similar abilities and to move ahead at their own pace and in their own way in order to grow to their fullest potential.

Other advocates point to special programs provided to children with learning problems. Special education for students with learning disabilities or cognitive delays exist because there are children who, despite the best efforts of qualified teachers, just cannot function in a regular program without focused support. Because of the way these students process information, they need to have the curriculum presented differently. They may need to have concepts or skills broken down into smaller steps, or they may need more repetition, explanation, and structure in order to learn. And there are those who are so different cognitively from the norm that they may need to be in a totally different classroom, where a different and more relevant curriculum is taught.

In the same way, the learning needs of many gifted children are so different from the norm that they need special support to stay challenged, motivated, and to develop their unique abilities.

What's Right for Your Child?

Sometimes the decision to place a child in a gifted education program is a simple one. And sometimes, it's not so easy. Maybe your child will need to be moved to a different classroom, or to a totally different school. Or maybe you've heard things from other parents that aren't exactly strong endorsements of the program you are considering. If you're struggling with making a decision, you are not alone. One place to begin is by asking yourself what you want your child to get out of school.

Most parents want their children to:

- Enjoy school
- Have access to great teachers and a supportive school staff
- Be motivated to do their best
- Have the opportunity to reach their full potential
- And have friends

If enrollment in a gifted program can help your child with these goals, then it's probably a good move. If she's already succeeding in these ways, then the choice is not so critical.

Below are some more specific questions to consider if you're deciding on whether a gifted program is right for your child.

Are your child's needs being met right now?

Gifted programs exist to support students who need a different kind of learning experience - where they can work at an accelerated pace, on an advanced level academically, and be around others with similar needs. If your child hungers for more stimulation and her teachers are having difficulty modifying the general education curriculum to challenge her sufficiently, then the move to a gifted program may be just what she needs. However, if your child is already thriving in her school program - that is, she is engaged, challenged, learning, and doing great socially - there may not be a pressing need to try something different. Some experts believe that children whose IQs measure in the lower end of the gifted range can thrive in either a general education classroom or in a gifted program: they can swim in both seas. It is often those whose IQs measure higher who truly need special support in order to be sufficiently challenged and engaged, and to find and connect with others who have similar interests and abilities.

It's also true that some children with high IQs are disorganized or unfocussed. Such children may do better in a highly structured general education classroom with a teacher who carefully plots out the curriculum and moves students along at their own ability level in a sequential, ordered manner. This type of child may feel lost in a gifted program where students are expected to organize their own learning and work more independently.

It's really a matter of considering your own child's learning style and needs in relation to the gifted program you're considering.

Will being involved in a gifted program help your child when he gets to high school or applies for college?

Being identified as gifted may allow your child to have access to special programs or more advanced-level classes in middle school, junior high, or high school. But, because it is easier to meet all children's learning needs with more schedule choices at the secondary level, separate gifted programs such as resource rooms or self-contained classes that may have been available at the elementary level may not be offered in many secondary schools. Formal gifted programs may be replaced by honors or advanced placement classes, and enrollment in these programs may be more dependent on the student's performance (grades, test scores, teacher recommendations) than on whether they've qualified for a gifted program in the past. Many secondary schools combine high-achieving students with identified gifted students in these classes, and then base continued enrollment on the student's performance, whether or not the student has been identified as gifted.

As far as college application is concerned, being identified as gifted can work both ways. Some college admissions officers may give special consideration to applicants who have been served in a gifted program. Others might set higher standards for students who identify themselves as "gifted" on their college applications - or they may be turned off if they feel the student is displaying an elitist attitude by flaunting their gifted label. Colleges are more likely to be interested in what the student has accomplished - the academic rigor of courses taken, college entrance exam achievement scores, performance in scholastic or extracurricular activities - than in whether the child has participated in a gifted education program.

Who do you think a typical college admissions officer would choose?

- ➤ A student who identifies himself as gifted who didn't use his potential and skated through school, taking the least challenging classes and just getting by with average grades.

- ➤ Or an "average" student who demonstrated a strong commitment to his education by taking challenging courses, getting outstanding grades, and showing excellence in extracurricular areas like sports, music, or volunteer activities?

47

Still, if participation in a gifted program in secondary school helps keep your child engaged and interested in her studies, allows her access to advanced placement classes, and consequently enhances her grades, test scores, and college resume, then there is certainly a benefit.

Check with someone knowledgeable within your own district about the benefits of having your child participate in a gifted program at the secondary level. A junior or senior high school counselor may be a place to start. A knowledgeable high school guidance counselor can also give you some insight into how participation in a gifted program might influence a college application screener at a specific college your child is considering.

What's the teacher like?

To a large extent, the teacher is the program, so get to know the gifted program teacher's style, personality, and philosophy. This may be the one time in your child's school career when you get to decide who his teacher will be, so make the most of it. Make an appointment and ask questions like: "How do you run your classroom?" "What kinds of things do you do differently in your class than in the general education classes?" and "How do you handle discipline?" Let the teacher know if there's anything unique about your child that might help him evaluate whether the program would be a good fit. For example, your child might like to work alone, be very "active," prefer using a word processor, or have a hard time spelling. Chances are that the teacher has had experience with other gifted students with similar issues.

Also, to better inform your sense of the teacher's style, make an appointment to observe the class. Check out the atmosphere, the kinds of activities the students are doing, the way the teacher interacts with the class, and any projects or student work displayed around the room.

48

What are your child's feelings?

Don't ignore your child's input when considering placement, especially if it may involve a change to a different school away from friends. When our own children were heading off to middle school we had a choice between two campuses. One was perceived as being more academic, while the other was viewed as more social. My wife and I were planning on sending our children to the academic campus, thinking that this would give them an advantage when they got to high school. But they had their mind set on the other campus where most of their friends were going. We relented and enrolled them there. Looking back, I'm glad we did. They still did well academically, but were also able to stay with their friends and maintain a positive attitude towards school.

As a school psychologist, one of the main criteria I use when placing children in any special program is their comfort level with being there. I let the child visit the classroom so I can see how they react to the teacher, the program, and the other kids in the room. Most children have a good sense of what they need and where they belong.

This is an approach that you can use too. If possible, let your child visit the teacher, group, or class that they may be working with. See what they say and how they react - and how the teacher reacts to them. Most districts encourage parents and their children to make such visits.

> Gifted Education Programs are sometimes called GATE or TAG Programs (or some other such acronym). GATE is an acronym for Gifted And Talented Education while TAG is an acronym for Talented And Gifted.

What does your child's current teacher think?

Ask your child's current teacher, or anyone else at the school who knows your child well, for an opinion. If they are familiar with the gifted program, they should be able to give you the inside scoop and tell you if they think your child would be a good match.

Are there any possible negative effects of a gifted placement?

Some of the issues you may want to consider include:

- Would your child need to be moved to a different school - away from his group of established friends or favorite teachers?

- Would your child have to miss important activities going on in her classroom during the time that she is pulled out to participate in gifted program activities?

- Is the program an additional time commitment (more homework, more large projects due) that may stress your already-stressed-out child?

- Would the type of instructional approaches used in the program complement your child's learning style?

What's your gut feeling?

Once you have gathered all the information you can about your district's program, sit back and get in tune with your instincts - your parent radar - and see what it's telling you. Go with that instinct, and remember:

Your Decision Doesn't Have to be Permanent

If you decline to enroll your child in a gifted program, take heart that many districts will let you change your mind down the line, should things change. And if you do opt to enroll your child, also know that the placement doesn't have to be permanent. You could think of it as a trial, and present it to your child that way, saying something like, "Let's try this for a year and see how you like it." If the end of the year comes and you find your child is overwhelmed, missing her old friends, and generally miserable, you can request that she be moved back into the regular program.

So, go with your gut, and if it doesn't pan out, make a change - isn't that the way life works, anyway?

Gifted Program Options

The type of program your child has a chance to participate in will be limited by what the district or school has to offer. Some districts offer only one option, while others offer a choice. Some let individual schools run their own programs, others centralize all programs at one or two sites - an approach which often requires that children be transported to a school outside their neighborhood.

Is one type of program better than the others? Not necessarily. The worth of any program will depend on the teacher involved, the support she is given, and the needs of the child. Those who are doing well in a general education classroom and are able to make social connections there may do better in a pull-out program where they are spending only a portion of their time with a group of other identified kids. Those who are totally out of place, socially and academically, in a regular class might do better in a self-contained gifted education room where they spend more time in a modified curriculum around other kids with similar interests and abilities.

Making educational choices is really a matter of seeing what's available to you, and then making the best decision you can with the information you have at the time. Also keep in mind that your child is a developing, evolving creature whose needs may well change over time. What works one year, may not the next. Be flexible, expect change, and go with the flow.

Out-of-Grade Placements

These programs involve moving a child into a higher grade level so that he can have access to an advanced curriculum and to academic peers. One benefit of these programs is that it doesn't cost the district much money to set up. For this reason, out-of-grade placement options may be used more frequently by smaller school districts with limited resources. Out-of-grade placements may also be used in combination with other programs.

Grade Skipping (or Whole-Grade Acceleration)

Children are moved ahead one or more grades so that they are learning with older students. Doing so allows gifted children to spend the entire school day in a curriculum more in tune with their cognitive abilities. Such an approach may be used for highly gifted children or for those working more than a year above their current grade placement in all areas who need more challenge than part-time or pull-out programs offer.

Of course, a potential disadvantage of grade skipping is that the child will have less time during the school day to socialize with those in her own grade. Some parents make up for this by having their children participate in after-school groups. Sports teams, scouting, and religious or volunteer groups are just a few of the avenues parents use to give their children the chance to hang out with kids their own age.

Early Entrance (or Acceleration)

Children start kindergarten or to move up to middle school, high school, or college before the standard age. Again, this alternative is usually reserved for the highly gifted who crave intellectual stimulation that they can't get in their age-based school program. Most cases of early enrollment involve students moving up through the system just a year or two earlier than normal. But we've all heard through the media of more unusual cases, like a seven-year-old enrolling in high school, or an eleven-year-old entering college. Skipping several grades in one swoop is sometimes called "radical acceleration."

Individual Subject Acceleration (or Concurrent Enrollment)

Rather than being moved ahead to a full-time placement in an advanced grade, some gifted kids spend only part of their day with older students for advanced instruction in specific subjects where they need the extra challenge and stimulation. For example, a third grade student will go to a fifth grade class for math instruction for part of the day. Or a junior high school student will take an advanced literature class on the high school campus through a special arrangement between the schools. These programs can work well for the many gifted children who show highly developed talent in only one or two particular areas.

Grouping

The out-of-grade placement options reviewed above might be thought of as taking the child to the curriculum, while the grouping options described below are more a case of bringing the curriculum to the child. Grouping involves placing students together with other gifted kids around the same age and using an advanced curriculum or special teaching techniques to meet their special learning needs.

Ability (or Cluster) Grouping

Gifted children are grouped together in a general education classroom for special projects or for subjects like math, reading, or science. This allows the teacher to provide them with advanced materials or higher-level activities, or move them along at a more accelerated pace. Grouping also addresses the gifted child's social needs by allowing them to spend time with one another and have an opportunity to form lasting friendships.

Ability groups can be temporary - put together for different units of study throughout the year and then disbanded when that unit is completed. Schools may also form permanent ability groups. For example, all children who have been identified as gifted in a certain grade may be placed with the same teacher, so that they can form a lasting ability group within that room.

Team Teaching (or Teaming)

There are two common models of team teaching. The first can be viewed as ability grouping across classrooms. Using this approach, two or more teachers structure their day so that they are teaching core academic subjects during the same time period. Then, through some type of formal assessment, they separate students in their classrooms into ability groups. For example, if two teachers are teaming for reading instruction, they may find that among their students there are four ability groups - one remedial, one at grade level, one a year above grade level, and one two or more years above grade level. This last group may include students who have been identified as gifted learners. Rather than each teacher forming four ability groups within their own classroom, each takes two groups, trading students across classrooms, depending on what type of instruction they need.

This approach models collaboration and allows teachers to spend more time providing lessons and activities that meet each student's particular needs. It also gives teachers a chance to work with the kind of student they are most skilled at reaching. A teacher who is trained in providing corrective instruction may choose to take the remedial group. Similarly, a teacher who has experience with enrichment and accelerated teaching could take the advanced students.

A second model of team teaching involves two teachers working together within the same classroom to plan and deliver a lesson or a series of lessons on a certain topic. The teachers collaboratively present a whole-group lesson and then work separately with individual "breakout" groups of students who are working at different ability levels, or on different aspects of the lesson. The groups may then come back together for a whole-class discussion of the group activities.

Resource Room (or Pull-Out) Programs

Gifted children are removed ("pulled out") from the general education classroom for a certain period of time each week and placed in another room where they work with other gifted children. The resource room program is usually taught by a teacher with special training in gifted education who is skilled at differentiating curriculum and providing activities that engage advanced learners.

A potential complication of these programs is that the resource teacher and the general education teacher need to work together to schedule the gifted child's resource room instruction at a time when other important activities or lessons in the general education class won't be missed. A benefit is that such programs allow gifted children who may be in different classrooms to connect with one another and form friendships. Since pull-out groups usually meet only once or twice a week, these programs may be combined with other options, such as ability grouping within the regular classroom.

Self-Contained Classrooms

Some districts provide gifted learners with a full-day gifted education program through enrollment in a special classroom with a specially trained teacher. These teachers typically use alternative education techniques throughout the day (see the Ways of Teaching section, below) to meet the needs of their students. Even though all students enrolled in these programs have likely been identified as gifted, teachers may still use ability groups and differentiated instruction to address students' relative strengths and weaknesses.

These programs can provide a more appropriate learning environment for highly gifted students than part-time solutions like ability grouping or pull-out programs. One potential drawback is that, because there are usually not enough gifted students to form a classroom on any one campus, self-contained classrooms may only be offered on one or two campuses within a district, so many students participating in these programs will not be attending their neighborhood school.

Ways of Teaching

The following teaching techniques and practices can be used in any classroom but are particularly suited to advanced learners.

Compacting (or Telescoping)

Students are tested at the beginning of a unit of study to see what they have already mastered. The teacher then "compacts" the material by allowing them to skip concepts or skills they already know so that they can focus on new and more challenging topics or projects that are based on their advanced learning needs. Sometimes students themselves are involved in the selection of the substitute curriculum or projects and sometimes it's left up to the teacher. This method helps students avoid useless repetition and provides more time for meaningful enrichment activities.

Thematic Instruction (or Brain Based Learning or Integrated Instruction)

Rather than teaching subjects such as reading, science, and math in isolation, teachers present these skills in the context of long-term units of study based around a central theme or concept. For example, for a six-week thematic unit on the rain forest, students may read and discuss books on that ecosystem, design and carry out scientific experiments based on topics such as photosynthesis, and develop and solve math word problems dealing with endangered species and deforestation.

Some researchers believe that students learn more naturally and efficiently when they see the interconnections between different subject areas and are able to apply what they learn toward real-world situations or problems.

Enrichment

Concepts are covered in more depth than usual. Enrichment activities may include reading a wider variety of books, gaining additional perspectives on an opinion, or doing independent research.

Pacing (or Acceleration)

Material is presented at a faster pace to complement the student's ability to process and master information quickly. Units of study that typically take a semester to present in a general education classroom may be covered in a month or two.

A Focus on Critical (Higher-Order) Thinking

Instead of asking students to memorize, define, or explain a concept, teachers focus more on higher-order thinking tasks, such as having students apply what they've learned to new situations, form hypotheses based on previous knowledge, or defend an opinion derived from their understanding of class material.

Individualized Instruction

A student's learning objectives and activities are based on their own learning needs, rather than on a predetermined set of standards.

Independent Study

Students are allowed to have input into what and how they learn and conduct their own research with little or no interference from a teacher. For example, an eighth-grade student who has mastered the state standards in biology independently studies topics of interest such as evolution or cell reproduction. The student may also use resources such as the internet and multimedia computer software to design a presentation in this area for the rest of the class. The teacher might support the student by providing access to the resources she needs and offering help along the way, while allowing her to work at her own pace and pursue her own ideas.

Cooperative Learning Groups

Students work in small, temporary groups on a specific project or activity. Each student in the group is typically given a different role (for example: leader, recorder, time-keeper, and presenter) and the group is required to work cooperatively. The group has a common learning objective which they are responsible for meeting, and students may receive a common grade for their group effort. Cooperative groups can be used along with whole-group instruction. For example, after a whole-class lecture on the solar system, a class may be broken into nine small groups with the goal of researching and developing a five-minute presentation on each of the planets.

Advocates of cooperative grouping believe that this model teaches teamwork rather than competition, and better reflects the way that students will eventually be asked to work together in their jobs or careers.

Learning Contracts (or Learning Plans or Individual Education Plans)

Teachers write down a student's learning objectives in a contract which also defines how they will be assessed on the attainment of their goals. The student is often allowed to collaborate with the teacher in determining the learning goals and assessment criteria that will be formalized in the plan.

Contracts allow students to work independently and at their own pace, while providing structure and a way to check progress against learning objectives. Contracts can be written for individual projects, lessons, or units of study - or they can be created for longer periods of time.

Portfolios

The teacher and the student collaborate to collect samples of the student's work in a certain area. The samples can be arranged in sequence and used as an assessment tool to evaluate a student's progress over time.

Portfolios are sometimes used as a more meaningful and authentic way to evaluate students' achievements and guide their progress than traditional grades or test scores.

Alternatives to Public School Gifted Programs

For parents who choose not to have their children participate in a district's gifted education program, or whose high-achieving or otherwise talented children do not meet the district criteria for these services, there are many other ways to nurture a child's gifts and talents.

Home Schooling

Many advocacy groups associated with gifted education endorse home schooling for kids whose needs aren't being met by the public schools. Some note that home-schooled children do as well as or better than traditionally schooled kids when they move on to college, and that many concerns about socialization opportunities are unwarranted. They point out that parents who home school have the opportunity to be more selective in who their children hang out with and therefore the kind of socialization that takes place. There are an abundance of books and websites that offer advice and educational materials for home schoolers. Many parents are surprised to learn that formal support for home schooling may also be provided through the local school district or through the local county department of education.

Private Schools

Many large urban areas have private schools that are specifically designed to serve gifted students. Some have strict entrance criteria that may include an IQ test score above a certain cut off point. These programs often work best for highly gifted kids who need to be immersed in an academically stimulating and challenging environment throughout their school day. This option can be expensive of course. Some private schools offer reduced tuition or full scholarships to families who can't afford the fees. Private schools in your area may be located through local family-oriented publications, an internet search, or a look through the phone book.

Magnet Schools

Magnet schools are campuses within a district that base their curriculum around a central theme or philosophy. Common themes include visual and performing arts, classic literature, technology, math, and science. Typically, students throughout the district are eligible to apply for these programs, with entrance based on a set of criteria which might include test scores, an evaluation of a student's portfolio, performances, and teacher recommendations. These programs are ideal for students whose interests or gifts are in the specific area associated with the theme of the magnet school to which they are applying. Some districts also have magnet schools for the gifted which may serve both formally identified gifted students and high-achieving students who meet other standards.

Summer University Enrichment Programs

Families who live near a college campus can look into having their child participate in a summer college enrichment program. Many colleges offer such programs for school-aged children and teens in areas such as writing, music, computer programming, and math.

For parents looking for a more intense summer enrichment experience, *talent search programs* offered by select universities across the country provide academic enrichment "summer camps" for bright learners. These programs generally have strict selection criteria which may include an IQ test score, teacher referrals, or out of level academic performance tests. Popular talent search programs include the Center for Talented Youth at John Hopkins University, the Center for Talent Development at Northwestern University, the Talent Identification Center at Duke University, and the Belin-Blank Center for Gifted Education and Talent Development at the University of Iowa.

Talent search Programs can be expensive. However, some offer reduced tuition or scholarships to those that qualify.

Mentoring

Children with a special interest in a certain field or occupation can spend time with an adult who is involved in this area. For instance, kids with a fascination for astronomy might "intern" for a professor at a local university for a few weeks during the summer. Children who are interested in medicine might shadow a local doctor once a week over the course of several months. These experiences might be arranged by parents or teachers who ask their friends or colleagues to act as mentors. Alternately,

61

adults could help a child seek out his own mentor through a campaign of research, letter writing, and phone calls.

After-School Enrichment

Parents may enroll their children in private after-school lessons or enrichment programs in place of, or in addition to, the gifted services offered at school. For children gifted in nonacademic areas like art, music, drama, or dance, private lessons or community recreation programs may be the only way to provide them with the advanced level of instruction that they need or desire. For academically gifted students, private learning clinics, or private individual tutoring after school hours may serve as another layer of enrichment in their areas of strength.

Distance Learning Courses

Distance learning - also called online learning - courses are a great way for parents to provide a sequential, structured, and challenging curriculum as part of a home school program, or as a way to supplement a traditional day school experience. Some of these programs cater to the special needs of bright, motivated students and require an IQ score or other entrance criteria for enrollment.

Some popular distance learning programs include the Education Program for Gifted Youth at Stanford University, the Hewlett-Packard Telementor Program, and the online courses offered though the John Hopkins University Center for Talented Youth.

CHAPTER THREE

What is Gifted Education?

Quick Points

- Gifted programs are designed for children who need special support and a different kind of school experience in order to stay engaged, challenged, and excited about learning.

- Whether participation in a gifted program is right for your child will depend on many factors, such as the match between your child's learning style and the program being offered, and the skills and philosophy of the teacher involved.

- Children with IQs in the upper extremes of the gifted range are more likely to need an alternative education program to stay academically engaged and challenged. Those who are more moderately gifted can often do well in either a gifted program or a general education program.

- Some districts offer only one type of gifted education program while others offer several options.

- Common gifted program options include:

  Out of Grade placement

  Which includes:

  Grade skipping
  Individual subject acceleration
  Early entrance

  Grouping

  Which includes:

  Ability grouping
  Team teaching
  Resource rooms
  Self-contained classes

- Teaching techniques for gifted learners may include:

> Compacting
> Thematic instruction
> Enrichment
> Faster pacing
> Individualized instruction
> Independent study
> Cooperative learning groups
> Learning contracts
> Portfolios

- Some parents of gifted, high-achieving, or artistically talented children opt for alternatives to enrollment in public school programs which may include:

> Home schooling
> Private school placement
> Enrollment in magnet school programs
> Enrollment in summer college
>   enrichment programs
> Mentoring
> After-school lessons or tutoring
> Distance learning courses

Chapter Four

IQ Testing and Gifted Education

Answers to the Questions Parents Ask Most

What score is needed for placement in a gifted program?

Generally, a child needs a full-scale IQ score that is in the 98th percentile or better to be considered gifted. This means that a child's score has to be higher than 98% of those in the sample on which the test was developed. On most IQ tests this means a score of 130 or higher.

Do all districts use this same cut-off score?

Many do, since an IQ score in the top two percent is a commonly accepted criterion for giftedness. However, keep in mind that in most districts an IQ test score is only one criterion out of several used when considering placement in a gifted program. A child who doesn't quite make the cutoff may still be placed if she meets other selection criteria like high achievement test scores or strong teacher recommendations. See Chapter Three for a more complete description of other selection criteria that districts may use.

Do districts always use the full-scale score when making placement decisions?

The full-scale score takes into account more aspects of intelligence than subscale scores and is considered to be the most reliable score obtained on an IQ test - the score that is most accurate and least likely to change. For this reason, many districts use the full-scale score when making placement decisions.

However, there are occasions when districts will use subscale scores in place of the full-scale score. For example, if the child has limited English skills, it would be unfair to base a placement decision on an IQ score that was lowered due to language barriers. In this case, placement decisions should be based on IQ scores that are not affected by verbal ability. In fact, districts that serve a large population of students from non-English-speaking backgrounds may make it a policy only to consider the nonverbal sections of an IQ test for all students they test. These districts may also use a nonverbal, individually administered IQ test - such as the Ravens Progressive Matrices or the Universal Nonverbal Intelligence Test - in place of a comprehensive individually administered IQ test when testing for giftedness.

On the other hand, verbal subscale scores may be used in place of the full-scale score for children with visual problems. Nonverbal IQ subtests often involve tasks like putting blocks together to match a design, or figuring out a pattern in a series of pictures. A child's performance on such subtests will be affected by a problem with vision. A child has to be able to see what he is doing and interpret what he is seeing in order to do well on these tests. A child who is visually impaired, or a child with a learning disability in a visual-perceptual area, would be at a disadvantage on these tests. In such cases, the child's verbal IQ subscale scores would be a better gauge of ability, and would likely be used in placement decisions.

Nonverbal subtests also often involve fine-motor ability - the test taker needs to move things around with his hands. Verbal subtests involve no such motor tasks. So, verbal subscale scores may also be used when testing a child who has a fine-motor disability.

Is the score my child received on a group IQ test likely to be similar to the score she receives on an individually administered IQ test?

Group tests are typically highly correlated with individually administered IQ tests - meaning that those that do well on one generally do well on the other. Yet, the scores are not likely to be identical.

They could be different for a number of reasons:

➤ Group tests may measure fewer aspects of intelligence. For example, in order to be fair to children who speak English as a second language, some districts choose to give group tests, or sections of group tests, that primarily measure nonverbal skills. A child with a strength in this area is likely to do well on such a test, even if she has relatively weaker verbal skills. However, if the same child takes an individually administered test which measures both verbal and nonverbal skills, her score may not be as high, since her verbal skills will be factored into the results.

➤ A child may do better on an individually administered test because of the individual attention he receives. Some children, particularly those who have problems with attention or organization, may benefit from having someone there to help them focus or provide extra support and encouragement.

➤ Kids with good reading skills have an advantage when taking a group test since they may need to independently read and understand test questions. Those who are behind in reading, or those with a learning disability in reading, will have a hard time working independently on such tests. These children may have a higher score on an individually administered IQ test where questions are asked orally by the examiner.

➤ An IQ score is going to differ from test to test, no matter how highly correlated the two tests are. In fact, even if someone takes the same test on two different occasions, the scores will almost certainly be at least a little different. Why? Because all tests contain error. Scores will be affected by a variety of conditions, including how the examiner administers the test and how the child is feeling on that particular day.

It is also true that group IQ tests may under-identify gifted children, significantly underestimating the IQs of those at the upper extremes of giftedness.

Reasons for this include:

➤ Gifted children may find the group testing experience uninteresting, and therefore tune out and not do their best.

➤ Gifted children might read too much into test questions, coming up with creative or novel answers that may be correct, but are not scored as such due to the strict objective scoring criteria used on group tests.

➤ Some group tests have lower "ceilings" - or highest possible scores - than some individually administered tests. If a gifted child bumps against that ceiling by topping out on several subtests or sections within the test, then her true IQ cannot be determined. For example, if the IQ score on a given group test only goes up to 150, there is no way for that test to truly measure the potential of a child whose IQ is actually much higher. It's like trying to measure a 7 foot basketball player with a four-foot tape measure - it can't be done.

Because group test scores are not perfect predictors of the score a child may get on the more reliable individually administered IQ test, many districts use group test results as only one criterion among several when selecting children for a gifted program or for further testing with an individually administered IQ test.

Why do schools wait until a child is in the second or third grade to start testing?

Most districts do not have programs for gifted children before this time, so there is no practical reason for schools to start testing at an earlier age. Also, earlier testing tends to be less reliable as some children's cognitive development is slower to come together than others. Any kindergarten teacher can tell you that at the beginning of the school year some kids arrive ready to learn while others are still in the preschool mode - they have trouble focusing, prefer to play alongside rather than with others, and are just not ready for a traditional school experience. Yet, by the end of the year, many of the less mature classmates have made great gains and are doing as well as some of the early bloomers. As time goes on, these variations in development tend to become even less pronounced. By the second or third grade children are more similar in terms of maturity and development and IQ scores are more likely to reflect the child's ongoing ability. In general, the older the child, the more reliable the IQ score.

Are there circumstances where a child should be tested before starting school?

There are circumstances when it is better to test a child at an earlier age, even with the understanding that early developmental differences may make the score less reliable.

Two reasons you might want to get an earlier assessment are:

➥ Your young child is showing signs of giftedness and you

want to confirm her IQ so you can consider placement in a gifted preschool or primary school program. Since most school districts do not start special programs for gifted learners until second or third grade, you'll probably need to explore private programs for such early intervention.

➤ Your child is showing early signs of giftedness and has also been showing signs of a behavioral or emotional problem, or has been having difficulty relating to other children her age. Such problems are not uncommon among children with high IQs. Characteristics of giftedness can be misinterpreted by overzealous or misinformed professionals as symptoms of ADHD, bipolar disorder, depression, or even a form of autism. While gifted children can certainly have these conditions, differentiating between gifted behaviors and the traits associated with such disorders can be tricky. The more information you and others have about your child's development, the better position you're in to identify the underlying causes behind any unusual behaviors. See Chapter Six for more on the potential emotional and social implications of giftedness.

Two common individually administered IQ tests used for children who have not yet reached school age are the Stanford-Binet Intelligence Scale and the Wechsler Preschool and Primary Scale of Intelligence.

Why is my high-achieving child not being considered for the gifted program?

There are lots of high-achieving kids who are better off in a general education classroom than in a gifted program. Gifted programs are designed for students who truly learn differently and need a different kind of school experience. So, how do you tell a high-achieving or bright child from a gifted child, without administering an IQ test?

You often can't, but here are some possible clues:

➤ Bright children often appear challenged and engaged by what's going on in the classroom and feel good about their classroom achievements. Bright kids often fit in well with others in the class too. They may enjoy working in groups and hanging out with others of their own age.

➤ Gifted children may appear bored or disinterested in the classroom curriculum. They sometimes crave more information or stimulation than the teacher can easily provide. Gifted children can also be perfectionistic and self-critical, always wanting to do more or learn more. They may also have a hard time connecting with other kids in the class, preferring to hang around older kids or adults.

Check out Chapter Five for more signs of giftedness. It's likely that your child was considered for the gifted program at some point, and that the teacher or others at the school concluded that she didn't fit the profile typical for gifted placement or for further testing. You might ask the teacher whether this is true.

Of course, there are lots of bright and gifted kids who don't fit the usual patterns. If you still think that your high-achieving child should at least be considered for the gifted program, ask that she be put through the formal screening process. Many districts will screen a child if a parent requests it. Once you have more information, both you and the teacher are in a better position to make an informed decision about placement.

My child was being considered for the gifted program, but didn't make it to the point where he was given an individual IQ test. I still think he would benefit from being placed in the program. What should I do?

Many districts use multiple screening methods to identify

students who are good candidates for an individual IQ test, then make a placement decision based, at least in part, on that score. Even if a child doesn't do well on one of the screening criterion, such as scoring high on a group IQ test, he might still be recommended for an individual IQ test if he meets other criteria such as exceptional grades and excellent teacher recommendations. See Chapter Three for other criteria that may be used in the selection process.

Yet, there are certain circumstances where the district's screening process may fail to identify a child who would be a good candidate for further testing.

For example:

- The child has difficulty paying attention in class. Students diagnosed with an attention-deficit hyperactivity disorder (ADHD) or other conditions which may lead to inattentiveness, such as depression or an anxiety disorder, may not do well on group IQ tests. These children often find it difficult to work in large groups, where there are more distractions and less opportunity for an adult to redirect them to what they are supposed to be doing. Consequently, they may perform poorly on a group IQ test and do much better on an individually administered test. Problems with attention may also affect classroom grades or performance on state achievement tests which are often used in the selection process.

- The child has not had a stable school history and his grades and school performance have been negatively affected. If a family has moved around a lot, or if a child has missed long periods of school for other reasons, then selection criteria like grades, teacher evaluations, and state

achievement test results may not truly reflect that child's
ability.

- The child is not engaged by the regular school curriculum
  because her learning style is not compatible with the
  teacher's approach or the general education curriculum
  itself - she is bored. Some gifted students are turned off by
  the sometimes repetitive nature of a general education curriculum. They may respond better to an alternative curriculum that allows them to move at their own pace and
  participate in more self-directed, creative learning experiences. Because they are not fully tuned-in at school, a
  teacher may misinterpret poor school performance as being
  due to a lack of ability, and therefore not recommend them
  for consideration for a gifted program.

Many (but not all) teachers are able to look at each child's
circumstances and pick up on their potential, despite some of
the conditions described above. If for some reason the teacher
is not aware of special circumstances that may have affected
your child's performance in the screening process, then schedule
an appointment and offer a little background. Perhaps with the
new information the district will agree to administer the individual test.

If you continue to feel that your child has been overlooked,
you may want to consider private testing. However, keep in mind
that it is up to the district whether or not they will consider outside assessment. For those that do, some will simply accept the
private test score while others may want to validate the score
with their own follow-up assessment.

What should I tell my child if she has questions before the test?

Answering your child's questions will help "demystify" the testing process and allow him to go into the test session feeling more relaxed, focused, and positive.

Here are some things to keep in mind when answering your child's questions about the testing process.

- ⟍ Be Calm and Confident. If you feel anxious about the test - possibly because you want your child to do well - he will almost certainly pick up on these feelings, which may create some unneeded anxiety. Some children (and adults) are already predisposed to being a little nervous when they know they are being tested, and seeing you act this way will not help. Your child may pick up more from your demeanor than from what you actually say.

- ⟍ Give Honest, Open Answers. Answer all of your child's questions, using age-appropriate language, and let your child know when you don't have the answers.

- ⟍ Just Provide the Information that Your Child Wants to Know. Most younger children will have few, if any, questions about the testing process. Most children just want to know what to expect.

Three common questions kids ask, and examples of answers you might give, include:

"What are we going to do?" "You're going to work with someone at school - I think they are going to ask you to do things like put puzzles together or work with blocks. They might also ask you some questions."

"Why am I doing this?" "Your teacher wants to see how you learn best, to understand the best way to teach you."

"How long is this going to take?" "Probably an hour or two"

Of course, some kids will want more specific information, and you'll need to adjust your language according to the age of your child. Consider letting your older or more inquisitive child look through this book on her own for the specific information she is seeking.

Is there anything I should do to prepare my child before taking the test?

Not really. Just keep routines as normal as possible. Be sure that your child gets plenty of rest the night before, and eats a good meal - just as you would on any school night when you want him to do his best. Avoid going out of your way to "prep" your child by doing things like having him get two extra hours of sleep or giving him an impromptu pep talk. He may interpret this as pressure to perform, which could create undue anxiety.

Where will the test be held?

The psychologist will typically set up a room that is free from distractions, with a small table or work area where he and the child can sit across from each other.

Do I stay with my child when the test is given?

Not usually. Typically, the examiner will greet parents, let them know about how long the test will take, and then take the child to the room where the test will be given. In rare cases, such as when a child is extremely anxious or fretful, a parent may be allowed in the room for at least part of the test session in order to reassure the child. However, this is really up to the examiner, or to district policy if there is one. Because the questions asked during an IQ test are closely guarded, many examiners feel reluctant to have a parent near enough to hear what is being said.

How long will it take?

Individually administered IQ tests take between one and two

hours to give, with most taking about an hour and a half. The time varies depending on how many responses the child gets correct (the examiner stops testing when a child misses a certain number of questions) and how quickly she responds.

When will I know the score?

There are generally three ways that scores are reported, depending on the policy of the district or maybe on the preference of the examiner.

- Some examiners will score the test immediately after the test session and then meet briefly with both the parent and the child (or just the parent, depending on the examiner's or parent's preference) to go over the results.
- Some examiners prefer to score later and then contact the parent by phone or mail with the results.
- Some districts ask the examiner to give the score to another district representative who then makes contact with the parent to review the test results.

What if I don't want to know the score?

The IQ test score that your child receives is just a snapshot of her performance on that particular test, at that particular time. Also keep in mind that your child's true IQ score can never really be known - just estimated. There is always some error in an IQ score. It's also true that IQ tests measure only a very narrow aspect of human ability, not even touching on important traits such as social skills, motivation, and self-awareness. Knowing this, you might choose not to be told the score so that you can watch your child's gifts and abilities unfold without any potentially misleading notions about her capabilities or limitations.

Rather, you might ask just to know whether or not your child met the district criteria for the gifted program. After all, that was the purpose of the test in the first place. If you want more information, you can also ask to be told what range your child's scores fell into - average, above average, and so on - or, more importantly, what the test results say about your child's relative strengths and weaknesses. For example, did she do better in verbal or performance areas? How was her memory? This kind of information can give you insight into your child's learning style and interests. And it's sometimes interesting to see if your own observations about your child, gathered over many years, match the examiner's test findings.

If my child is tested again in a year or two, is the score likely to be the same?

IQ scores tend to be reasonably stable after age seven or so. If a child is tested with a well-recognized IQ test in second or third grade, and again at ten or eleven, the scores are not likely be identical, but within a fairly tight range - within ten points or so.

This stability in scores is probably due to the following reasons:

- ➤ Cognitive development in younger children can appear to be uneven, with periods of apparently slow development followed by periods of sudden gains in areas like attention, motor ability, reading, and understanding number concepts. But once children reach age six or seven, most of the neurological puzzle pieces are in place, and it's less likely that there will be many major changes in ability.

- ➤ IQ tests measure traits that are influenced by both our experiences and our genetic endowments. While new experiences can lead to improvements in the skills measured by IQ tests, our underlying genetic makeup is relatively fixed.

- ➤ Even though environmental influences - such as greater

access to learning experiences and mentoring from an adult - can positively affect a child's IQ score, most children's environments do not change that much from one year to the next.

Of course, while on average IQ scores tend to be fairly consistent, it is possible that an individual child's IQ score can be quite different from one test to the next. Large differences (more than ten or fifteen points) may occur when a child doesn't do his best on one of the tests due to poor test conditions, or when a child is immersed in an ideal learning environment between tests. For instance, studies have shown that children from impoverished backgrounds who are adopted into homes that provide lots of love, attention, and learning opportunities can make sizable gains in IQ. See Chapter Ten for more information on environmental and genetic influences on ability.

How accurate are IQ scores?

While all test scores contain some element of error, the score on a competently administered IQ test given after age seven or so should be pretty accurate for most children.

However, IQ scores can significantly underestimate the ability of some gifted children due to the effects of test "ceilings." When administering an IQ subtest, the examiner will stop testing when the test taker has correctly responded to all the test items or has made a certain number of errors - for example, missing four out of five consecutive responses. Extremely gifted children may hit the ceiling, or "top out," on several subtests because they answer all the questions correctly or because they do not miss the required number of responses before the end of the subtest. When this happens, the child receives a high score on those subtests, but there is no telling how high the scores would have been if the child had gone farther. The child's abilities are beyond what can be measured by the test. If the child tops out on two or more subtests, then the full-scale IQ score is best viewed as a low estimate of the child's ability.

Most IQ tests are simply not designed to accurately assess the abilities of children in the extreme ranges of giftedness. To get a better IQ estimate in these cases, the child would need to be tested by a private practitioner trained in the use of tests designed specifically for children and adults with unusually high IQs. There are reports of gifted children who score 50 or more points higher on these specialized tests than on the IQ tests more commonly used in the schools.

If all tests contain error, how can I know my child's true IQ?

The score that a child gets on an IQ test is called an *obtained score* and should only be thought of as an estimate of her true ability. According to statistical theory, the only way to know a child's *true score* would be to have her take the test over and over, dozens of times, and then find the average of all of the scores. In reality, however, this can't be done because the child is likely to do better on the test each time she takes it due to a practice effect.

So how sure can we be that an obtained IQ score is a good estimate of a child's ability? Fortunately, test manufacturers have a way of estimating the amount of error associated with a certain test for a child of a given age. They then use this information to provide test administrators with tables of *confidence intervals*. A confidence interval is a range of scores likely to contain a true score. This range can be large or small, depending on how certain you would like to be.

For example:

➤ The psychologist administering your child's test may report that the full-scale IQ score is 97 and that the confidence interval associated with a 90 percent degree of certainty is 93 through 101. That is, you can be 90 percent certain that your child's true score is somewhere between 93 and 101.

➤ Similarly, he may report that that the full-scale IQ score is 97 and that the confidence interval associated with a 95 percent degree of certainty is 91 through 103 - meaning you can be 95 percent certain that the true score is somewhere in that range.

Again, the more certain you want to be that the true score falls within the confidence interval range, the bigger the range needs to be.

Not all psychologists will report confidence intervals. If yours doesn't, and you'd like that information, just ask. It's likely that the examiner can look it up for you quickly if the test manual is handy.

Do districts take confidence intervals into account when considering cut-off scores for gifted education programs?

Districts usually just use the child's obtained score when looking at eligibility. Of course, it's understood that all tests contain error, but the obtained score is still seen as a good estimate of ability - and that's all an IQ test does, provide an estimate of learning potential.

Also, keep in mind:

• Error works both ways. Your child's true score is just as likely to be slightly lower than her obtained score than higher. To account for this, districts would actually need to raise the cut-off score for placement, say from 130 to

135, to be more certain that children's true scores fell into the gifted range.

- All standardized test scores contain error - your child's score and every other child's score. Everyone is in the same boat, so using the obtained score gives no particular child an unfair advantage.

My child took the test and I don't think she was at her best, that day. Should I say anything?

There are situations that might negatively impact your child's score. Of course, the best thing to do is to make the examiner aware of these conditions before the test session begins. If your child is sick or on a medication that may decrease her alertness, for example, let the examiner know right away. It is possible that he will want to reschedule the test for a time when your child is feeling better.

Even if you are unaware of something that may impact your child's test performance, examiners are trained to look for such conditions during the test session. For example, they will observe the child to see if he appears ill, inattentive, excessively nervous, and so on. If an examiner notices something that is likely to affect the test outcome, he will often note this and discuss it with you when reporting the score. He should also report this information to district representatives who are in charge of interpreting test scores and making placement decisions.

If the testing has already occurred and you feel there was something in particular that you or the examiner missed which may have impacted your child's performance, bring it up for discussion. The district can use this information when considering how to interpret your child's score. Someone may suggest that a second test be administered at a later date, in order to validate the score on the first test.

Remember, however, that in most districts the IQ score is only one of several criteria used to determine whether a child might benefit from a gifted program. In some districts, children whose IQ scores meet the district criterion may not, in the end, be found eligible for the gifted program, since they did not also meet the other criteria. On the other hand, some students will be found eligible even if they score below the cutoff on an IQ test since they have met the other criteria.

For more information on other selection criteria used for gifted program placement see Chapter Three.

I still think the score is inaccurate. Should I get a second opinion?

Paying for a private assessment is always an option. But again, first ask your district representative if they accept outside testing. Some districts do not.

Another alternative is to wait until the following year - or whenever the next round of testing has been scheduled - and ask that your child be retested at that time. At this point, too, it may be good to step back and look at your own motives. If you find yourself getting stressed out over your child's IQ score, or over whether or not she qualifies for the gifted program, it's likely that she will pick up on this and start to feel that stress herself. Bear in mind that many children whose IQ measures in the moderately gifted range (130 to 145) can thrive in a general education program. See Chapter Two for more on how to determine if a gifted program is right for your child.

How much will it cost to get a private assessment?

The price will vary from one examiner to the next. You should probably expect to pay between four hundred and eight hundred dollars for an individually administered test which includes a follow-up report. Some psychologists will charge by the hour, so their fees will vary a bit from child to child. Others will charge a flat fee for the test and report.

Who is qualified to administer IQ tests and how do I find them?

IQ tests are typically administered by a clinical or educational psychologist. While a clinical psychologist is licensed to provide therapy to the general public and to administer certain tests, many of them do not have much practical experience with IQ testing, as this may not be a large part of their practice. If you decide to hire a clinical psychologist, make sure that he or she has an extensive background in administering IQ tests to those in your child's age group.

Educational psychologists usually have more experience at administering IQ tests to school age kids.

Private practitioners can often be found in the Yellow Pages, in local family-oriented magazines, and through web searches. You might also check with other parents for a reference.

What kind of IQ test should I ask for?

Ask for a comprehensive (measures both verbal and nonverbal areas) individually administered IQ test, such as the most recent versions of the Stanford-Binet Intelligence Scale for Children or the Wechsler Intelligence Scale for Children. These are among the most widely recognized comprehensive tests in the field for school-aged kids.

If my child qualifies for the gifted education program in our district, does that mean she will qualify for this program in another district if our family moves?

Not necessarily. There are no federal laws regulating how districts identify students for gifted programs. Some districts immediately place a previously identified gifted student in their own gifted program at the parent's request, while others require additional testing before doing so.

This is not true in the case of children with disabilities since there are federal laws governing how districts identify and serve these students. If your child is identified as having a disability which qualifies her for special education services then wherever you move in the country the new district must immediately honor the previous evaluation and provide the same services.

PART TWO

Giftedness and Kids

CHAPTER FIVE

Signs of Giftedness

What To Look For and Why You Should Know

Schools are often able to identify gifted students by using the screening methods outlined earlier in this book, so when it comes to discovering if your own child is gifted, one option is to wait to see whether teachers or others at your child's school recommend testing for a gifted education program.

Yet, you shouldn't be entirely dependent on the schools when it comes to identification. Keep in mind that many teacher training programs require little (if any) course work in giftedness, so some teachers and school administrators may not have all the information they need to recognize gifted children. For this reason, your insights are important, and the more knowledge you have, the better position you're in to partnership with others when selecting the best programs for your child.

In fact, parents should become familiar with the signs of giftedness even before their child starts school. Most school districts do not even start identifying children for gifted programs until second or third grade, and parents of exceptionally bright or gifted children may want to consider private testing or alternative placement options (such as a private preschool gifted program or early grade acceleration) before that time. Early testing and identification can be a controversial subject, but many advocates of gifted children believe that they should be identified as soon as possible so that their unique needs and talents can be acknowledged and nurtured right from the start.

Early identification is also important when a young child is showing behavioral or social differences - not fitting in, being highly focused on unusual interests, appearing more distractible or inattentive than others of the same age - and parents want to understand the cause. These characteristics may be features of giftedness or may be signs of an emotional problem or such conditions as Attention Deficit Hyperactivity Disorder (ADHD) or Asperger's Syndrome. Knowing a child's IQ can allow insight into a child's atypical development and help to avoid potentially harmful misdiagnoses.

Under-Identified Children

Some gifted children may not be particularly high achievers in the classroom. These students may have problems with attention (which may or may not be related to ADHD), have poor organizational skills, or simply not "mesh" with the teaching style in the classroom, and therefore may be overlooked when it comes to selection of gifted program candidates.

I recall one boy I tested privately at the request of his mother. The boy, Mike, was in the fourth grade at the time. His mother was concerned because Mike was getting poor grades, having conflicts with the teacher, and becoming more and more disinterested in school. He was having social conflicts too, being teased and picked on by other students who liked to see his "overreactions" when they provoked him. It had gotten to the point where home schooling was being considered since it was getting harder to even get Mike out the door to go to school, which he considered "torture."

The school had never tested Mike for giftedness. Whatever screening process was in place had missed him. Possibly because he didn't fit the high-achieving, cooperative, wunderkind image that some teachers look for when making recommendations for gifted screening. Yet it turned out that his IQ measured in the 160's - in the exceptionally gifted range. His problems at school were not atypical for such children. Had he been identified earlier and placed in an alternative program, many of his academic and social problems might have been avoided. At the very least, Mike's parents and teachers would have had a better understanding of his problems and been able to collaborate from a more informed perspective to come up with solutions.

These types of scenarios are not unusual. In fact, some estimate that the majority of gifted children in the schools are never identified. That may not be a tragedy for some, but it very well could be for others like Mike who truly need special programming and support to get through school successfully.

Parents who are aware of the signs of giftedness can better collaborate with the schools to help assure that their own child's potential and learning needs are not overlooked.

How Can You Tell if Your Child is Gifted?

As you've probably guessed, without proper assessment, there is no easy answer. There are no universally accepted traits that you can look for and no definitive signs that will tell you for sure whether your child is gifted. However, many gifted children share some common characteristics, and knowing these is a good place to start.

The reason for these common traits may have a lot to do with the physical characteristics of the brain. Giftedness is the result of both environmental and genetic factors, and both of these influences can lead to differences in the way the brain works and develops. Some researchers believe that gifted children's advanced cognitive skills actually result - at least in part - from the ability of their brains to process information faster and more effectively than others their age.

The brain is made up of billions of nerve cells, or neurons, which communicate with each other by releasing and receiving chemicals called neurotransmitters. These chemicals travel through dendrites, root-like structures which branch out and seek connections with nearby neurons at junctures called synapses. The more of these dendrites and synapses we have, the greater our "brain power" - our ability to process information, to perceive, interpret, reason, problem-solve, remember, and do all kinds of tasks associated with learning. It appears that every time we do or experience something - read a book, have an emotion, look at a picture - a specific group of neurons associated with that activity "lights up," stimulating the growth of more dendrites and "exercising" those already in place, making them better processors of information. All else being equal, the denser and more efficient these neural connections, the easier it is to do the thing that is associated with that area of the brain.

Gifted children's abilities may be related in part to these enhanced neural connections, either because:

- They were born with a denser than normal thicket of neural connections associated with the traits in which they are gifted, and had the right kind of experiences to allow them to use and retain, or further develop, these connections; or

- They were born with a *sufficient* amount of neural connections and had ample opportunity to form more and more efficient connections through an enriched environment.

The denser, more efficient neural connections shared by gifted children could help explain the common characteristics many of these children share. But keep in mind that not every gifted child will show all, or even most, of these characteristics, and some will show traits that are quite contrary to what you might expect in a gifted child. It's commonly known that Albert Einstein learned to speak at a late age and didn't read until he was seven. Gifted children can be as different from one another as they are from the rest of society.

If you've ever learned a musical instrument, you probably have a good sense of how this process of "exercising" and building neural connections feels. I recall learning to play the guitar and just how difficult it was for me to form chords at first. I struggled to place each finger on the right string, in the right pattern for each new chord. Each time I needed to change to a different chord, I had to stop and spend a minute or so painstakingly rearranging my fingers into the new positions on the fret board. But after a while, forming chords became easier - my fingers moved faster, and I was able to switch between chords without having to stop and think about each finger's position. The neural connections were there, as a result of my experiences - my practicing. The same thing happens when you practice a golf swing, learn a mathematic operation, or develop a mental ability such as meditation.

In the rest of this chapter, I'll review some traits that gifted children may possess. In the next chapter, I'll go over other traits shared by some gifted children which may lead to negative outcomes. But keep in mind that trying to identify gifted children by comparing their behaviors and traits against lists such as those presented in this book can be tricky. After all, many or even most children will show a lot of these same characteristics. The most important thing to do when considering your own child is to look at him or her in the context of other children of the same age. If there are consistent, noticeable differences, then advanced mental abilities may be present. Another clue may be that others - friends, relatives, teachers, neighbors - notice and comment on the same traits that you're seeing.

Language Skills

While most children are able to form recognizable sentences and understand complex language by about two years of age, gifted children often reach these milestones earlier. As they approach school age, other language skills may appear advanced or sophisticated.

Some of the traits of giftedness to look for when considering your child's language development in relation to others of a similar age include:

- A highly developed vocabulary and the ability to learn new words easily.

- The tendency to speak quickly.

- The early use of longer, more complex sentences while using appropriate grammar.

- Early reading, if given some instruction and opportunity. Many gifted children have already learned how to read before entering school.

- Continually asking questions about what they see and hear, and wanting to receive thorough responses and explanations.

- The ability to understand and carry out multi-step directions at an early age. (e.g., Go to the dining room, get the blue book on the table and put it back on the shelf in your room, then bring me the clothes on your bed so I can wash them).

- The ability to understand and participate in adult conversations. Gifted children often pick up nuances or double meanings early on - so watch what you say!

- The ability to change the language they use when speaking to different audiences. For example, a four-year-old gifted child might use more advanced words and sentence structure when speaking to adults or older children, and then talk in a simpler, more childlike way when addressing his three-year-old cousin.

Learning Abilities

All children (all people really, big and small) have an inborn desire to learn about the world around them - to seek out new experiences, figure out the relationship between themselves and their surroundings, to discover, and to learn. What distinguishes gifted children from others is the apparent natural ease and joy with which they go about doing this. Their brains appear to be mental sponges, effortlessly absorbing and incorporating new information and ideas.

Many gifted children are natural learners who show some of the following characteristics:

- The ability to learn quickly and efficiently - to pick up ideas and skills effortlessly.

- A tendency to become highly focused on certain areas of interest (e.g., bugs, space, animals) and independently seek out information on these topics.

- The ability to ask questions that show advanced insight or understanding.

- A deep fund of knowledge - they know more about the world around them than you would expect.

- Excellent memory and easy recall of what they previously heard, saw, or learned.

- A tendency to read often on their own and to frequently prefer reading to more physical activities.

- Little need for direction or instruction when beginning a new activity, learning a new game, or acquiring a new skill. They may also insist on doing things on their own, or in their own way.

- Early development of motor skills involving balance, coordination, and movement. Gifted children may also be advanced in some purposeful fine-motor activities such as assembling small objects (e.g., legos, transforming toys, blocks) or putting puzzles together. However, other fine motor skills may not be advanced. Some gifted children are poor at handwriting - although this may be more related to a lack of attention to detail or impatience with the slow and tedious task of handwriting practice than to problems with fine motor control.

- Pleasure in talking to older children and adults about topics that interest them.

- An understanding of their own thinking and learning processes. They may have preferred ways of learning and resist using other methods suggested by a teacher or adult.

They are able to sense how much and what kind of studying they need in order to master a skill or topic.

- Creative thinking. Gifted children may enjoy coming up with their own ways to solve problems and take delight in complexity and making connections between seemingly unrelated ideas or concepts.

- The ability to concentrate on a topic of interest for an unusually long period of time. However, gifted children may quickly shift their attention or appear unfocussed when doing something they perceive as unchallenging or uninteresting.

- An inclination to see learning as fun. They take joy in discovering new interests or grasping new concepts.

Despite having a high IQ, some gifted children do not shine at school early in life, and may only wake up to their potential later- in high school, in college, or even as older adults. But, take heart! This can sometimes work in their favor. Kids who feel pressured to excel early on - either by their own perfectionist attitudes or by an overly insistent parent - can become exhausted or burned out by the time they are of college age. And late bloomers who become self-motivated through an "Aha!" moment (Like, "Aha! I better get off the couch and get serious because Mom and Dad aren't going to pay my bills anymore... ") can often make up for lost time by attacking their goals with a fresh burst of intellectual energy, creativity, and a renewed sense of purpose.

Emotional and Behavioral Traits

Gifted children are often more emotionally intense than others. They can also be more sensitive to others' feelings and circumstances and may display a great deal of empathy in situations where others their age appear indifferent.

Other emotional or behavioral traits to look for include:

- A high activity level. Gifted children can appear to have an endless source of energy - constantly moving, talking, asking, and exploring.

- The tendency to think and talk fast. Because they may be trying to speak as quickly as they think, gifted children are often asked to "slow down" so the listener can understand them. They can also become frustrated when they feel that others are talking too slowly, or taking too long to "get to the point."

- Strong leadership qualities. Gifted kids often make natural leaders who take charge and lead others in new directions.

- Ability to relate to older kids and adults. Because their cognitive skills and interests can be advanced for their years, gifted kids have an easier time connecting with and learning from those older than themselves.

- Enjoyment of alone time. While gifted children may enjoy spending time with others, including mental mates (whether their own age or adults), they can also enjoy spending time on more solitary activities such as reading, writing, daydreaming, observing, or just thinking.

- Appreciation of natural beauty and art. Gifted children may particularly enjoy being around and pointing out trees, sunsets, flowers, the ocean, animals, and other things of inherent beauty. They can also show a deep interest in certain forms of art - paintings, sculptures, or music, for example.

Hidden Gifts

Some gifted children show only a few of the signs listed in this chapter, or show traits that are quite the opposite of what you'd expect. For example, some will start to speak late rather than early, some will be emotionally reserved rather than intense, and some appear to think and speak slowly rather than quickly.

Also keep in mind that there are children who show gifted qualities when it comes to language or emotional traits, but who do not appear exceptional when it comes to learning or academics. While some of these kids may have a specific learning disability (see Chapter Seven) getting in the way of their performance at school, others may have learned early on to hide their abilities in order to better fit in with others their age, or to avoid the pressures of higher expectations.

Many high-achieving or gifted adults show few signs of giftedness early on in life. Albert Einstein wasn't the only genius who didn't exactly shine in childhood. Thomas Edison, Isaac Newton, and Winston Churchill all had trouble early on in school. Countless others, famous or not, have been misperceived as "slow" or worse in childhood, only to go on to accomplish amazing things later in life. How can we explain this? We can't always. It may be that these late bloomers were products of uneven or delayed neurological development - their brains took a little longer to get all the "wires" connected in just the right way. Or it could be that the signs were always there but were masked by other aspects of giftedness - such as distractibility or nonconformity - which made it difficult for adults to see beyond to the child's true talents.

And of course there are children who show many of the signs listed in this chapter who do not measure in the gifted range once they are tested. Does that mean they are not gifted? Not necessarily. Many kids don't shine on IQ tests due to test anxiety - or sometimes because of the very qualities associated with giftedness. For example, IQ tests typically have timed subtests, meaning that the faster a child responds or correctly completes a task, the more points she earns. However, gifted children who are perfectionists may respond more slowly than others, taking their time, working carefully and methodically, and checking their responses for accuracy. A gifted child with a high energy level who has a hard time focusing attention on structured tasks may also be at a disadvantage when it comes to performing in the rigidly structured atmosphere of an IQ test.

In addition, it's true that children can be gifted in one area (verbal skills, for example) but show only average ability in others (such as perceptual or nonverbal reasoning skills, which are important for math achievement). While these children's full-scale IQ score might not measure in the gifted range, they may still demonstrate some common traits of giftedness. For example, a verbally gifted child with average nonverbal reasoning skills may still be emotionally sensitive and have an excellent memory.

Identifying giftedness can be tricky, particularly regarding those who test right around that "magic" cutoff point of 130 or so. And IQ tests are certainly imperfect instruments and only one piece of the puzzle. Your insight and instincts, along with those of your child's teachers, can often be the most important pieces needed to truly understand your child's unique gifts and potential.

CHAPTER FIVE

SIGNS OF GIFTEDNESS

Quick Points

- As the primary advocates for their children, parents should be just as informed as teachers and others in the schools when it comes to understanding the signs of giftedness.

- Since schools typically do not start IQ testing until second or third grade, parents should be particularly aware of early signs of giftedness. Early identification of giftedness is important when parents are considering alternative preschool education options, or when a young child is showing behavioral or emotional problems which might be associated with giftedness and which could be misinterpreted - or worse, misdiagnosed and improperly treated.

- Many gifted children are overlooked by the schools because of problems with attention, motivation, or other issues. A parent who understands the signs of giftedness can help teachers and others see beyond these conditions and assure that their own child's potential and needs will not be overlooked.

- There are no "sure signs" that a child will measure in the gifted range on an IQ test. Gifted children can be as different from one another as they are from the rest of society. However, research shows that many gifted kids tend to show some common characteristics.

- The reason for these commonalities may have to do with how gifted kids' brains are "wired." Gifted children may have more, or more efficient, neural connections which help them to process information more quickly and effectively.

Signs of giftedness may include:

- Advanced language skills - including early development of language ability, a large vocabulary, and the ability to understand and participate in adult conversations.

- Enhanced learning aptitude - including the ability to learn new skills and concepts quickly and efficiently, a tendency to become highly focused in certain areas of interest, excellent memory, the capability of working independently, advanced motor skills in certain areas, and the ability to understand how to study effectively.

- Emotional and behavioral traits - which may include emotional sensitivity and heightened empathy, a high energy level, the tendency to think and talk fast, strong leadership qualities, enjoyment of alone time, and appreciation of natural beauty and art.

CHAPTER SIX

Is It Good To Be Gifted?

Optimal IQ and the Flipside to Being Gifted

Is it good to be gifted? This may sound like a strange question - of course being gifted is good, isn't it? It's true that kids who score higher on IQ tests will generally do better academically. After all, these tests are designed to predict school success. The skills tapped by IQ tests, including memory, problem-solving, and language ability are also important for doing well on college placement tests, succeeding in a career, and accomplishing every-day tasks like figuring out your taxes or organizing a PTA fund raiser. So there's definitely an upside to being gifted. But how gifted do we need to be to reap these benefits - and is there a flip-side to having a high IQ?

Optimal IQ

It may seem reasonable to believe that the higher our IQ, the better off we are. Yet, it turns out that's not necessarily true. Those with higher IQs will have an advantage over those with lower IQs, all else being equal, when it comes to ease of learning and having the cognitive skills necessary to succeed in certain careers. However, researchers have found that beyond an IQ of about 120 there is little relationship between IQ and personal achievement. (And please note that an IQ of 120 does not even meet the cutoff for gifted education programs in most districts.) Beyond this level, achievement appears to be related more to things like creativity, leadership ability, and personal motivation than to IQ. Those with extremely high IQs (in the 145 to 180 range, for example) do no better than those with IQs in the 120s when it comes to career success and creative accomplishments. And having a higher IQ is certainly no guarantee that you'll zip through life effortlessly accomplishing great things.

I've seen this myself. I've met many people who don't appear to be particularly bookish or intellectual, but are very successful in what they do. Then again, I've known lots of academic types who have scored extremely high on an IQ test but lack the "people skills," personal motivation, or whatever it takes to translate their abilities into outward signs of success - a college degree, a rewarding career, a fulfilling family life.

Maybe you've noticed this, too. Consider people you know and admire for their accomplishments - those who make everything look easy and always seem to be getting ahead. It's likely that these people are not all "brainy" types. Rather, most are probably of average intelligence but know how to use their abilities to connect with and lead others, to stay focused on their goals, and to work hard to get what they want.

Of course, that's not to say that those with an exceptionally high IQ won't do well in life. Many do, and some of them contribute great things to our society in part because of their unusually high intellectual ability. An exceptionally high IQ may also be useful, or even necessary, in certain professions that require more isolated cerebral types of work, such as theoretical physics or mathematics.

So what is the optimal IQ? It's arguable, but some would say around 120 and no higher than 145. Why? At this level, you'd reap most of the advantages of having enhanced abilities in some areas but might be spared some of the potential downside of being too "different" from the rest of the world.

The Flipside to Having a High IQ

Just as it's unfair and unrealistic to make generalized statements about any group of people based on similar traits they share, we shouldn't oversimplify our view on the effects of giftedness on children. In fact, having a high IQ doesn't necessarily come with any particular disadvantages. The research in this area is mixed, at best. And much of it is based on interviews or anecdotal evidence, which makes it hard to come to any firm conclusions about the findings.

Yet, all children are susceptible to struggles at some time in their development and gifted children are no different. A common belief is that they are more prone to certain developmental problems due to being perceived as different by others, or because they see themselves as being out of touch with most of their peers. And this makes sense. A primary need of most kids - and maybe, to a lesser degree, of most adults as well - is to "fit in." Anyone who's been through school understands how important it is to dress like, act like, and be like everyone else. Or at least like everyone else in your own little subgroup. We seem to have a need to be folded into a crowd with whom we can share certain interests - a social connection, an identity. Yet gifted kids are, by definition, different, at least when it comes to certain skills or talents they possess. Yes, giftedness is arguably a positive difference - at least from an adult perspective - but a difference, nonetheless. For kids and teens, the pressure to conform is often so great that any deviation from the norm can be distressing. We've all heard terms like brain, nerd, geek or worse applied to kids who seem too bookish, or too "into" school.

In support of the idea that an extremely high IQ is not a necessary condition for great achievement, researchers have found that many accomplished scientists, Ph.D.'s, college professors, and medical students have IQs that measure below that magical cut-off point of 130. The famous physicist and Nobel laureate, Richard Feynman, was said to have an IQ that measured around 125. What does this tell us? What we already know - that IQ tests are imperfect instruments that only measure a narrow band of our abilities and talents and may totally miss out on capturing the true essence of our potential.

Of course, the potential for social problems is not unique to gifted kids; all children are susceptible to teasing, bullying, or social isolation when they don't fit in, for whatever reason. The school years can be tough for all children. Gifted kids, though, do share some unique pressures and developmental issues that others may not.

A Disconnect Between the Brain, the Body, and Emotions

Most six-year-olds look, act, and think like six-year-olds. They use six-year-old words, think six-year-old thoughts, and react emotionally like you'd expect a six-year-old to react. Gifted children, however, are often described as showing "asynchronous development." That is, while much of their development may be typical for their age (their size and emotional reactions, for instance), cognitively they are out of sync. Gifted children's advanced cognitive skills allow them to process what's going on around them at a different level than most of their age peers. An outcome of this is a sophisticated and heightened curiosity about what's going on in the world, and a desire to "fill in the gaps" of their understanding.

All children are curious about the world and how it works. But for most, their curiosity is satisfied by simple, concrete answers that allow them to move on to other thoughts and emotions. They may see adults as the experts and not feel a need to question or seek elaboration on the answers provided by them. Gifted children, however, may not be satisfied with simple answers. These children often have a need to delve deeper to satisfy their advanced awareness and heightened curiosity.

For example, while most young children who lose a family pet may be satisfied with parental reassurance such as, "Your hamster is going to Heaven to live with his friends," a gifted child may not be content with such a simplistic response and want more information before moving on: "What is Heaven?" "Why do we have to die?" "Will you die someday?"

Gifted children may also have a tendency to want to discuss "adult" issues - such as death, spirituality, and the afterlife - at a deeper, more involved level than most kids their age. Other potential topics may include sexuality, birth, money, relationships, and divorce. While discussing these types of issues calmly and openly is not necessarily detrimental to a child, there can be drawbacks. A child who is excessively concerned about these things may become overly focused, frightened, or "grossed out" by knowing too much about issues they lack the life experience or emotional maturity to fully understand.

A seven-year-old whose father loses his job, for instance, may become anxious because he knows enough to understand the potential negative outcomes associated with the lack of a steady income. He may be concerned about the possibility of having to move out of his neighborhood, or not having enough money to get by. A five-year-old who knows "where babies come from" may find the whole subject so fascinating that he shares his expert knowledge with all who will listen.

In short, there is a certain bliss in the innocence of childhood that may be lost on gifted children who are enlightened too quickly concerning life's mysteries.

Emotional Sensitivity

Gifted children are often thought to be more emotionally perceptive and responsive than their peers. Some people have described them as having finely tuned antennae when it comes to picking up and responding to emotional signals that come from within themselves or from those around them. The reason for this extra sensitivity may have to do with physical differences in the brain itself.

Those who excel on the skills involved in IQ testing may do so because their brains more quickly and efficiently process the skills and knowledge required for such tasks. The exact reason for this efficiency is unknown, but, as you've read, it likely has something to do with the density of connections among brain cells and the efficiency with which these connections are able to manage information through chemical and electrical messages. In other words, doing well on an IQ test has much to do with the way the brain is "wired" through a combination of genetic and environmental influences.

It may be that the abundant neural connections responsible for these children's increased "brain power" also predisposes them to be hypersensitive emotionally.

Some researchers have reported that gifted children may:

- Be overly empathetic to other people's problems or situations. They might show a tendency to make the problem their own, and mirror the moods or emotional state of the person they are concerned about.

- Overreact to frustration, rejection, success, or any situation that triggers an emotional response: for example, sobbing over an outwardly minor disappointment.

- Be overly sensitive to criticism or disapproval, or respond strongly to minor suggestions or comments about their work or performances.

- Worry too much about global situations such as poverty, war, and natural disasters over which they have no control.

- Read too much into other people's comments or body language.

Friendships

Friendships are often based on similarities. We tend to connect with others who are like us in some way. That is not to say that two people need to be clones of each other to bond - differences are often what make a relationship interesting and may be what initially attracts one person to another. But it's fair to say that long-term relationships are often kept going because the people involved are somehow similar. And arguably, mental similarities are one of the most - if not *the* most - important ways that people connect and stay connected. We tend to become close with those who think like us. Not necessarily people who have the same opinions or outlook, but rather those who understand our ideas and perspectives, share similar interests, and with whom we can carry on a mutually meaningful conversation. Children and teens form meaningful and lasting relationships in much the same way.

One famous study of gifted children was begun by Lewis Terman of Stanford University in the 1920s. Terman identified over 1,500 people, including many children, whose IQs measured in the gifted range. Then he, and other researchers after his death, followed them over time to see how their lives and careers developed. One reason he began this research was to disprove the "early ripe, early rot" idea. At the time, many people felt that there was a fine line between genius and madness, and that those who burned too brightly as children would flame out in the end. Terman's study had many flaws by today's standards. For example, instead of choosing his subjects randomly, he selected them mostly from white, middle-class families. And instead of remaining an objective observer, he became actively involved in some of their lives by giving them advice or writing them letters of recommendation. However flawed, the study has given us some of our earliest insight into what it means to be gifted, and more than 40 years after Terman's death the research continues, even though there are now relatively few Termites (as the subjects affectionately came to be called) living. One outcome was to disprove the "early rot" theory. Most of the gifted kids in the study did well as adults - many getting advanced degrees and leading apparently fulfilling lives. Yet it was also revealed that giftedness did not shelter them from the agonies of life. The Termites became alcoholics, got divorced, and committed suicide at about the same rate as everyone else.

A potential problem for gifted children is that they often think in a different way than most of their age peers, those they are likely to spend a great deal of time with. They have the physical appearance and probably the emotional maturity of their classmates, but may have the vocabulary, interests, and reasoning ability of those much older than themselves. They don't really fit into either group. Consequently, developing meaningful friendships can be more difficult for gifted children, and this problem can become more pronounced as cognitive ability increases. Put another way, the pool of potential same age "mental mates" shrinks as IQ rises.

As an illustration, let's say that kids are more likely to form close connections with others who measure within 15 points (higher or lower) of themselves on an IQ test. Using a standard score to percentile conversion table (like the one provided for you in Chapter One), we know that:

- If a child has an average IQ of 100, about two-thirds of her peers will have an IQ that falls within 15 points of hers.

- If a child has an advanced IQ of 120, a little more than one-third of her peers will have an IQ that falls within 15 points of hers.

- And if a child has a "highly gifted" IQ of 145, only about two peers out of one hundred will have an IQ that is within 15 points of hers.

We can see that, based on sheer numbers, those with an average IQ would be in a better position to find mental mates in their classrooms and neighborhoods than someone with an IQ of 120 - and certainly in a much better position than someone who scores in the stratosphere with an IQ of 145 or more.

Gifted children may also have a difficult time socially because:

- They may be perceived by others their own age as show-offs, bossy, or just plain weird: "... that kid's always reading and using big words!"

- The older children with whom they may connect with mentally don't want to hang out with them because of the age or social difference.

- Their vocabulary, abilities, or talents may intimidate others. We develop opinions of ourselves by comparing our abilities to others. Kids and adults who are less confident in their own abilities may feel uncomfortable when they compare themselves with someone they judge to be "smarter" or "brainy."

- They may be too intense emotionally, showing strong reactions or emotional neediness, thereby scaring off potential friends.

- Younger gifted children may believe that everyone should think the same way they do, and become upset when they are proven wrong. For instance, a gifted four-year-old child who is trying to explain the rules of a board game to a group of classmates may get frustrated when the other children don't catch on as quickly as she expects. Or a gifted child with an advanced sense of justice may feel personally offended when another child unintentionally bends a rule in a kickball game.

Avoiding such social isolation and providing children with the opportunity to connect with others with similar cognitive skills is one of the common arguments for promoting gifted education programs.

Self-Esteem

Self-esteem can be thought of as the opinion we hold of ourselves. So where do we get this opinion? As children, we begin to develop a mental picture of ourselves in several different areas, including how we look, how we act, how popular we are, and how good we are at learning. This mental picture is formed from early childhood through feedback we get from others and from comparing ourselves to those around us. The picture becomes clearer and more fixed as we get older, since our ideas about who we are get reinforced over time. As we mature, we also develop a concept of an "ideal person," or how we "ought to be." These ideas are likely formed through messages received from sources around us like our parents, teachers, peers, and the media.

Our self-esteem, then, comes from comparing our mental picture of who we are to who we think we should be. Our feelings about ourselves can differ greatly according to what area of our lives we are considering and how we measure up to the ideal.

While studies show that many gifted children have high global self-esteem (how they feel about themselves in general) and high self-esteem when it comes to academics, it is also known that they are not immune to having poor opinions about themselves. Self-esteem issues may be particularly troublesome for gifted children who are prone to perfectionism - the desire to do everything just right before one can be satisfied with the outcome. Realizing their own potential and capabilities, these kids may get the feeling that they should be able to do just about anything, and then become frustrated when they don't perform up to their own expectations. For example, getting less than perfect grades, not making the varsity sports team, or not winning an award for the best science project may make the gifted child feel that he has let himself down. Self-esteem may also be negatively affected when gifted kids feel that they are not measuring up to other high-achieving students, or to adult mentors whom they see as role models or intellectual equals.

Another potential problem is that, because of their advanced cognitive development, gifted kids become socially aware at an earlier age than most children, which may lead to early feelings of being different from others. Younger children lack the insight and maturity to understand or process these feelings and to put things into perspective, which could deepen emotions.

Having a gifted child can present social challenges for parents, too. Maybe we don't like to admit it, but most people, consciously or not, harbor some resentment or feelings of jealousy when they hear other parents talking up (or bragging about) their kids. Rightly or wrongly, people tend to evaluate themselves by comparing their lives and circumstances to those around them. When we hear others speak about their children's accomplishments, we may feel defensive about how our own kids are doing. Many parents of high-achieving or gifted children have learned to keep quiet about their kids' accomplishments, for fear of alienating their adult friends.

Depression

Gifted children who are not able to live up to their own unrealistic or perfectionist expectations, or those who feel alienated from the rest of the world because of their intellectual differences, may develop feelings of sadness or depression. This is particularly true for the highly gifted child or teen who may develop the sense that the world they live in is a foreign land where everyone thinks and acts differently than they do. As they get older, these children may begin to question the meaning of a world that is seemingly run by those whose values and interests are so different from their own.

Becoming caught up in academic competitiveness can also lead to depression and other serious consequences. It is known, for instance, that suicide attempts occur more frequently among young people who excel academically, are highly creative, and attend highly competitive schools.

School

The very traits that help gifted children excel in learning can make it difficult for them to participate in many school programs.

For example:

- Because they are usually able to complete tasks quickly, they may become disinterested in a subject once they feel they have mastered it, and then begin to tune out the teacher while they move on to different things in their own minds. These children may be perceived as unfocussed or as "daydreamers."

- They may be more focused on the big idea, rather than the small details of a school task or subject. The organization of their school work may appear to be lacking and attention to detail may be missing. They may be perceived as disorganized, inattentive, or defiant.

- They may not need as much structure and teacher guidance as most and prefer to guide their own learning and move at their own pace. Teachers may become frustrated with students who are always moving ahead or getting "off topic."

- Because they learn and complete work at such a fast pace they could spend much of their school day with little to do or nothing to engage their attention. Some become bored, apathetic, discouraged, or rebellious.

- Their thoughts may come faster than they can write - so there is often a disconnect between how they think and what they produce on paper. This could lead a teacher to group gifted children with students of much lower ability, thus frustrating the child further.

- Teachers that are not skilled at adapting their instruction to meet the needs of gifted learners may feel threatened by how quickly the child learns, or by how much they know. Such teachers may try to make the gifted child conform to the pace of the classroom through reprimands or discipline techniques that create hard feelings or a poor working relationship between the teacher and the student.

Energy Level

Gifted children often need a lot of stimulation and have many interests. Parents and teachers can get worn out trying to provide enough, and the right kind of, activities to keep the child engaged and challenged. The child may also become drained and exhausted by pursuing too many hobbies or interests at one time - they may go from one project to the next in a chaotic fashion, never really completing what they started.

Ways Kids Cope

Gifted children are as diverse a group as any other, and no two children are alike. How they navigate through the social world and cope with the stresses of growing up may have more to do with individual personality traits, or the type of emotional support they get from others, than with their IQ.

Yet there are some common themes when it comes to how gifted kids cope. Because of the social isolation and negative feedback they may encounter, there is some evidence that, as they get older and have more of these experiences, some gifted children start to downplay their abilities, becoming guarded or holding back when they are around children their own age. Others may disguise their abilities in other ways - like focusing on nonacademic-related talents, or simply choosing to isolate themselves from others kids, preferring to be alone or choosing the company of adults.

Many though, as they mature and gain the insight that comes from experience and maturity, learn to accept and appreciate their differences without any long-term negative consequences.

Whether or not a child is dealing with any of the issues outlined in this chapter, parents can help their kids through the school years by:

- Being there to listen, understand, and support them emotionally when they are going through a stressful period.

- Providing them with opportunities to develop and explore their interests and connect with others who hold similar interests.

- Avoiding pushing them to excel or compete - or excessively praising them for their accomplishments.

➤ Encouraging fun, playful activities and downtime.

Most importantly, research (and common sense) tells us that all children benefit from having at least one caring, supportive adult in their lives who provides structure, consistency, and a sense of unconditional love, warmth, and encouragement.

Reframing the "Problem"

Again, the research is mixed when it comes to gifted kids and social adjustment. Being gifted certainly does not mean that a child will have a rough time growing up. Many of the potential negative effects of a high IQ may never arise, particularly for those children who measure in that "optimal" range of around 120 to 145. Many studies have, in fact, shown that most gifted children are well-adjusted and have no more social problems than most.

It's also true that the denser and more efficient neural connections that some believe are related to gifted children's emotional sensitivity and other issues can also help them in social relationships. Many of the same characteristics that seem to create problems for some gifted children can lead to positive outcomes in others, and many of the possible drawbacks associated with giftedness can also be viewed as potential advantages.

For instance, highly developed sensitivity and emotionality may help gifted children develop social insight, enhance their capacity to understand and connect with others, and boost their ability to adapt to different social groups. Instead of causing them to overreact or have melt-downs over little things, being highly sensitive may allow gifted children to be more responsive to others' needs, and give them an advantage in reading others' body language, feelings, and emotions.

Similarly, having fewer social contacts, or true friends, could certainly be viewed as a negative aspect of giftedness. But for some children it may just mean that they are more discerning when it comes to choosing who they hang out with. And preferring to be alone at times does not necessarily mean the child is suffering from social isolation. Gifted children are often highly introspective, and choose to be alone to develop their gifts through solitary activities.

Other gifted characteristics with possible negative implications, such as boredom with school routines, bossiness, and questioning of authority, can also be viewed as early signs of an independent thinker or a natural leader.

CHAPTER SIX

Is it Good to be Gifted?

Quick Points

- A person does not need to measure in the gifted range on an IQ test to do well in school or in a future job or career. Traits like personal motivation, work habits, creativity, and perseverance can often make up for the lack of a high IQ when it comes to academic or career success.

- There is little practical advantage - and some possible liability - to having an extremely high IQ. Those with an IQ of 120 or so are likely to have all the cognitive skills they need to be successful at just about any academic or career field they choose, and are less likely to be affected by any potential drawbacks related to being too "different" from their peers. For this reason, some consider an IQ in the range of 120 to 145 or so as optimal.

- Because of their advanced cognitive skills, gifted children may want to explore and understand adult issues, or the "big questions," before they are emotionally mature or experienced enough to fully process the information they seek.

- Some gifted children are overly emotional or hypersensitive. They may display excessive empathy for others, overreact to criticism or any other situation that triggers an emotional response, and worry excessively about global situations such as war, poverty, and the environment.

- Gifted children - particularly those who are highly gifted - may also face complications in the area of friendships. Because of the relatively small number of gifted children in the population, some have a difficult time finding "mental mates," or those with whom they can connect intellectually to form long-lasting friendships. Problems with friendships can also occur because gifted children may be perceived as being bossy, show-offs, or too emotionally sensitive by other children.

- Gifted children who show perfectionist tendencies may also display low self-esteem in some areas. Used to excelling at most things, they may become frustrated or disappointed when they fail to live up to their own high expectations. Some even suffer depression.

- The very traits that help gifted children excel at learning - like being able to finish tasks quickly and wanting to explore ideas independently - may make it difficult for them to participate in a regular classroom.

- Because gifted children can be very active and have lots of interests, parents and teachers can become worn out trying to provide enough, or the right kind of, activities to keep them engaged and challenged. The child may also feel overwhelmed or stressed out by trying to keep up with too many activities at one time.

- Some children cope with the potential negative consequences of being gifted by downplaying or disguising their abilities, while others simply learn to accept and appreciate their differences.

- Many gifted kids will not experience any of the potential negative consequences associated with being gifted, and many of the "problems" that are common to some may in fact be advantages to others. For example, being highly emotional and sensitive may allow some gifted children to better understand and connect with other people. Also, potential negative traits such as "bossiness" and questioning of authority can also be seen as the early signs of a natural leader.

• Whether or not their child is gifted, parents can help kids cope by: being there to listen and offer emotional support; providing them with the opportunity to connect with others who have similar interests; avoiding emphasis on competition; encouraging fun, playful activities, and downtime; and providing structure, consistency, and a sense of unconditional love, warmth, and encouragement.

PART THREE

IQ Testing and Learning Disabilities

CHAPTER SEVEN

Bright Kids with Learning Problems
When IQ and Achievement Don't Match Up

When some parents think of high-achieving or gifted students, what comes to mind is a child who shines in every aspect of life - one who can be expected to get straight A's in school, have tons of friends, and be a star in sports. The idea is, if you're smart, you're smart, and you should be able to apply your mind and talents to just about anything and do well. Problem is, this idea just isn't true. Yes, some kids and adults do appear to know it all and have it all, but this is really more the exception than the rule.

And when it comes to academic abilities, most children, even those who are very bright or high-achieving, have a definite set of strengths and weaknesses. We all do. Think of your own school experiences. Were there classes or subjects that were easier for you - where you felt most comfortable and in your element? How do you learn best? Are you someone who needs to read something to understand it, or do you retain information better when you hear a lecture, or see a picture or a visual presentation? How about your child - does he or she breeze through certain subjects and struggle with others?

Some variation in abilities, including those involved in doing well at school, is normal - a fact that is consistent with many current views on human intelligence. That is, intelligence should be thought of as a group of distinct abilities, rather than a global or general factor that filters down to everything we do. One child may be great at art and reading, but not so great at math or athletics. Another child may be truly creative in the way he views the world or in the way he approaches problem solving, but have a hard time getting his ideas down on paper. In other words, intelligence is not one "thing" that we can point to, and just because you excel in one area doesn't mean you'll do as well in others.

For most of us, these differences are no big deal. We get through school and life by working a little harder at the things that don't come as easily, or we learn to compensate for our weaknesses by using our strengths. If we have a hard time understanding information that we read, we may use pictures or diagrams to help us learn, or we visualize the material in our minds. If our memories are weak, we might learn to take detailed notes, study more often, or develop other strategies to help us recall information. We learn, often unconsciously, to adapt.

For some children, however, the differences between their abilities are so great that it is difficult, if not impossible, for them to succeed in school just by working harder or through compensating. These children have a true learning disability - a persistent and obvious block when it comes to learning certain types of material. For some children, the problem may involve reading, for others math. Still others may struggle with written or spoken language. These are otherwise capable children who, even though they have had great teachers, help at home, and plenty of opportunity to learn, still don't seem to "get it."

What Causes Learning Disabilities?

No one can say for sure, but many experts believe that learning disabilities are the result of a neurologically based difference in the way that the brain processes information. These differences may have to do with the number, arrangement, and efficiency of neurons or neural connections in specific locations of the brain associated with the skills needed for reading, math, or whatever task the child is having problems with.

In some cases, there may be an identifiable cause for such brain-based problems, such as a seizure disorder, birth trauma, or head injury. However, in most cases there is no obvious explanation. It may be that the neurological irregularity was caused by some undetected event during pregnancy, child birth, or infancy, when the rapidly developing brain is particularly susceptible to injury through such things as a lack of sufficient oxygen or the presence of toxins. Alternatively, some learning disabilities may simply be the result of a genetically inherited difference in the way the brain processes information - a "trait" the child was born with. I've heard many parents of these children remark, "I was just like that when I was in school."

While most learning disabilities have no apparent underlying cause, some researchers have attempted to come up with an explanation for certain types of learning problems. One interesting theory was promoted by the neurologist Norman Geschwind and his colleagues, including Albert Galaburda. They noted that people who are talented in areas like art, music, and math are more likely than most to have language-related disorders such as stuttering, problems with reading, and even autism. This team also found that these people tend to be "non-right handed" (that is left handed, ambidextrous, or not show a strong preference for using either hand) and have more problems with conditions like allergies, asthma, or colitis - which are sometimes thought to be associated with an immune system disorder.

In an attempt to explain this unusual cluster of characteristics, Geschwind drew on brain research that shows that the two hemispheres of the brain are related to distinct skills and abilities. The right hemisphere, which largely controls the activities on the left side of the body, is more associated with spatial and nonverbal skills, including creativity and the skills involved in art and music. The left hemisphere mostly controls the activities on the right side of the body and is more associated with sequential skills like language, math calculation, and logic. The team theorized that some learning disabilities involving language may be related to a disruption in the normal development of the brain hemispheres caused by an elevated level of the hormone testosterone during pregnancy.

It has been observed that the left hemisphere of the brain is slower to mature than the right, and is therefore more susceptible to injury during development. Geschwind suggested that an over abundance of testosterone that occurs around the fifth month of pregnancy may act to slow the growth of brain cells in the particular area of the left hemisphere involved with language ability. When this happens, the brain compensates, making up for the damaged area by growing additional brain cells and neural connections in other areas of the brain - particularly in the left-hemisphere area associated with math calculation and in the right-hemisphere areas associated with spatial ability and performance in areas such as art and music.

This theory would explain why those gifted in math, art, and music tend to have more language-based learning disorders and why these people are more likely to be left handed. Since their right hemisphere, which controls the left side of the body, is more highly developed, they may have an easier time using their left hand for motor activities such as writing.

Adding more support to this theory is the finding that an over-abundance of testosterone during the fetal period can also affect the development of the thymus gland, which is believed to be related to the body's immune system. That may explain why this group of learning disabled children has more immune-system disorders than the general population.

If this idea is correct, the surprising implication is that some gifted people, including accomplished artists, musicians, and mathematicians, derive their talent, at least in part, from a brain "injury" caused by the affect of testosterone.

While Geschwind's theory may help to explain the presence of certain types of language-based learning disabilities in some otherwise high-functioning children, the direct origin of most learning disabilities may never be known. Yet, when it comes to children and learning disabilities, understanding the cause is not as important as being able to identify, early on, whether such a disability exists so that some type of support can be given to support school achievement.

What to Look For

Some signs that your child may have a learning disability are:

- He appears to be trying his best, but is still struggling in one or more subject areas despite having a skilled teacher and support from you at home.

- He shows a big difference in performance between subject areas - for instance, consistently doing well in reading and writing, but poorly in math.

- There are obvious signs of problems with cognitive skills like attention, memory, understanding or using language, or following directions, and these problems appear to be getting in the way of school success.

- He reverses letters and numbers much more often than others his age, or has a hard time recognizing words that he has seen repeatedly.
- He forgets what he has learned from one day to the next.
- His teachers are concerned about his lack of progress in comparison to other children of the same age or grade, or feel that he is working below his ability.

If your child is struggling in school and shows one or more of these signs, it's time to call an individual meeting with the teacher to discuss your concerns. Often, parents and teachers can find solutions together, without having to look any further. A modification of homework assignments, extra tutoring, or a change in ability groups within the classroom are some common solutions.

If you've already tried accommodations suggested by your child's teacher without success, go to the next step and ask for a *student study team* (SST) meeting (sometimes called a student intervention team (SIT) meeting, a grade level intervention team (GLIT) meeting, a brainstorming meeting, or some similar term). Schools typically hold these meetings when interventions at the classroom level are not working and there is a need to get other opinions about how to best support a child. The student study team is often made up of the child's general education teacher, other experienced teachers at the school, the principal, and sometimes a special education teacher or school psychologist. The team will listen to your concerns, discuss your child's strengths and weaknesses, and come up with recommendations that can be put into action by the general education teacher. These recommendations might include additional services during or after school, the use of supplementary learning materials, a change in the way your child is grouped for instruction, or suggestions about how you might provide extra support at home.

The kinds of remedial programs available to general education students vary from district to district, and often from school to school. Some schools have a general education learning specialist or special programs and materials available for students who need extra support. Some allow general education students to receive informal or "school based" support from special education teachers on campus. In these programs, students who need extra help are grouped with formally identified special education students for instruction in the areas where the support is needed. The instruction may take place in the general education classroom, or children may be pulled out once or more a week for instruction in a special "resource" room.

If your child is still not succeeding despite the best efforts of the teacher and the school team, and you or your child's teacher still believes that a learning disability may be present, then consider requesting testing for formal special education services. By law, schools have a certain number of days after receiving a parent's written request for testing to respond and develop an *assessment plan*, outlining what types of tests will be used. The type of tests chosen will likely be determined by a review of your child's records, observation, teacher comments, and information you provide. If your child is being tested, be sure to let the school psychologist know what you think the underlying problem might be. For example, if your child is showing signs of a memory problem or a short attention span, speak up now. The psychologist may only test in areas where a deficit is suspected, and your insight will help identify where that problem may lie.

Once the assessment plan is signed and received by the school district, the assessment team (which usually includes a school psychologist, a special education teacher, and sometimes other specialists depending on the child's needs) has a limited amount of time - typically about two months - to complete the testing and hold a meeting with the parent to go over the results and determine whether the child qualifies for special education services. In the next section, I'll go over the criteria that are used by some districts for qualifying students for such services under a learning disability condition.

Learning Disabilities and Special Education

Special education programs are designed for students who, due to an identified disability, need extra support or a specialized curriculum. Unlike gifted education programs which may have different entrance standards from district to district, special education is a federally mandated and funded program, and is therefore governed by a set of strict rules and regulations. The federal government dictates what types of students are eligible to receive special education services, and districts generally only serve those who meet these criteria. Reasons for such strict limitations probably have a lot to do with funding. There is only a limited amount of federal money set aside for special education services, and guidelines are in place to assure that only students with true disabilities - those who cannot learn or benefit from schooling without special support - have access to those funds.

Children in the following disability categories typically qualify for special education services:

- Learning disability
- Speech and language delays
- Cognitive delays (mental retardation)
- Emotional disturbance
- Autism
- Traumatic brain injury

- Physical or orthopedic impairments
- Visual impairments
- Hearing impairments
- Dual sensory impairments (deafness and blindness)
- Other health impairment (a medical problem that impairs learning)
- Multiple disabilities

Most bright kids with learning problems are served under the learning disability (sometimes called "specific learning disability") category, so we'll focus on this condition here.

While children with severe and obvious disabilities (like mental retardation or cerebral palsy) are often identified and offered special education services before entering kindergarten, those with more subtle learning disabilities are usually not identified until second or third grade, and often later. The criteria for special education services under a learning disability condition usually require that a child is not making progress in the general education program and not working up to his potential, and it often takes a few years before this becomes clear.

Learning disabilities can also be difficult to identify. While many children have trouble learning in school, not all of them can be said to have a learning disability. The term "disability" implies that there is something going on within the student that makes her unable to learn when given the opportunity to do so. A child might be having difficulties in school for reasons that have nothing to do with such an internal problem. Poor instruction, poor attendance, or a history of frequent moves or change of schools are some possibilities.

Learning disabilities are often hard to recognize because there is no obvious physical or behavioral problem to look for. Also, there is no single agreed-upon definition of just what a learning disability is or how to test for one. Whether or not a child qualifies as learning disabled is really a matter of what definition or criteria is used at the time. In fact, the whole concept of how to identify children with learning disabilities continues to be controversial. Some argue that the criteria for qualifying kids is often so vague that the whole concept is essentially meaningless - a student who qualifies for special education services in one district may not in the next, since different eligibility criteria may be used.

Still, by law all school districts must have a system in place for finding and serving those students who are learning disabled. Federal law gives states and districts some flexibility in deciding just how to do this; however, many districts use some version of a method that is often called the *significant discrepancy model*, or simply the *discrepancy model*.

To qualify for special education services under this model, an assessment team must find that:

1. There is a *significant discrepancy*, or big difference, between the child's ability (often as measured by an IQ test) and academic achievement.

2. There is a *psychological process deficit*, or problem with the way the brain processes information, which would explain why the child is not learning up to his ability.

3. And the process deficit is the main cause of the student's low achievement.

To better understand this model, let's look at each of these three pieces separately.

IQ Testing and the "Significant Discrepancy"

IQ tests measure many of the same cognitive skills needed for school learning. For this reason, one assumption of the discrepancy model is that a child's IQ score should roughly predict that child's scores on tests of academic achievement.

In other words:

• Children with high IQs should be able to get similarly high scores on tests of academic skills like reading, writing, and math.

• Children with average IQs should get average academic achievement scores.

• While children with lower IQs would be expected to score similarly lower on achievement tests.

The first step in assessing a child for a learning disability is often to administer an IQ test to get an estimate of learning potential. Next, one or more academic tests covering skills like reading, writing, and math are given to look at how well the child has been able to learn. The IQ test will probably be administered by a school psychologist, while the academic tests are often administered by a special education teacher.

Both the IQ test and the academic tests are *standardized*. That is, they are designed so that the scores can easily be compared to one another. To check for a significant discrepancy, a child's IQ score is compared to the scores obtained on academic achievement tests. If the scores in academic achievement are found to be near or above the IQ scores, it can be assumed that a learning disability does not exist - the child is learning at or near her potential. However, if the child's scores in one or more academic areas are far below what would be predicted by her IQ, then it can be said that a significant discrepancy, or big difference, between the scores does exist - the child is working far below what would be expected.

But how "significant" does the discrepancy have to be? The specific number of score points can differ one district to the next, but it is usually somewhere between 15 and 30 points. Many districts use a 15, 22, or 30 point difference between the scores as the criterion.

As an example, if a district is using a 22 point difference as the criterion:

- A child with an average IQ score of 100 would need test scores of 78 (far below grade level) or below in one or more academic areas before the difference was large enough to be considered a significant discrepancy.
- A child with an above-average IQ of 122 would need test scores of 100 (at grade level) or below in one or more academic areas to demonstrate a significant discrepancy.
- And a child with an IQ in the gifted range of 135 would need test scores of 113 (above grade level) or below in one or more academic areas to demonstrate a significant discrepancy.

As you can see, children with higher IQs can be working at or above grade level in academics and still be considered to have a significant discrepancy between their ability and their achievement - since they are not working up to their own potential as estimated by their IQ score.

If your child is being tested for a learning disability, find out what criteria the district uses. If the district is using the discrepancy model, ask how many score points are needed to establish a significant discrepancy.

Sometimes, children are told to "Act your age!" It often seems that adults also tell children to "Act your IQ!" That is, we have an expectation that a child with an average IQ should be getting at least average grades in school, a gifted child should be getting straight A's, and so forth. This idea seems to hold true for many kids. But think about it; IQ and school performance don't necessarily have to go together, even if a child does not have a learning disability and is perfectly capable of achieving at her IQ level. Having a high IQ or being able to score well on an achievement test does not mean that the child will necessarily apply that ability to getting good grades. Some children, or more likely teens, are just not "into" school, for whatever reason. They may be purposely choosing to downplay their abilities in order to fit in with their peers, or they may be focused on other interests or goals, and genuinely disinterested in achieving good grades. The good news is that many of these kids will eventually come around and live up to their abilities - that is, start acting their IQ. But for some it may not happen until they are young adults on their own and start to see the connection between the effort they put forth and their future goals.

Finding a Psychological Process Deficit

Once a significant discrepancy has been found, the assessment team needs to determine whether the primary cause of the student's underachievement is due to a true cognitive problem -

sometimes called a psychological process deficit, or simply a process deficit or processing problem.

While only one such deficit needs to be identified, in reality learning problems are likely to be the result of a complicated combination of deficits - or inefficiencies - in the brain. Nothing happens in isolation. Learning any subject takes a coordinated effort of many different cognitive processes. Reading, for example, involves taking in and making sense of visual symbols in the form of letters and words, and integrating this input with auditory information - sounds and combinations of sounds. Learning to read also involves skills like memory and attention. A child has to be able to focus and hold her attention on the page, the words, and any instruction given, and then hold the information in memory long enough to rehearse and absorb the new material.

A school psychologist or other specialist such as a speech and language therapist will usually diagnose process deficits through individual testing, observation, the use of rating scales, and clinical judgment. Often children are tested only in areas where a problem has been indicated through a review of the child's score profile on an IQ test, by observing the child in the classroom, or through parent or teacher comments on how the child learns. I'll review some of the common process deficits next.

Memory

Children with short-term memory problems may have difficulty with things like reading comprehension or following a detailed conversation since they are unable to retain information long enough to connect the thoughts and ideas they are reading or hearing to other ideas they have previously encountered. Memory problems can disrupt the flow of learning in many other areas as well. These children may have difficulty doing mental math problems that involve more than one step, and will need more frequent repetition and practice to remember simple math facts or become fluent in basic procedures like adding or subtracting with regrouping.

Signs of a memory problem that a parent can look for include difficulty learning basic math facts despite good instruction and frequent repetition, great difficulty retelling simple events in a story that has just been heard or read, difficulty understanding or following multi-step directions, problems with staying on topic in a conversation, and asking the same question several times within a short time frame.

Memory can be broken down into auditory and visual recall. While some children have a deficit in both areas, others may show weakness only in one and may be able to use their stronger memory system to compensate for their weaker one.

Attention

Another common process deficit concerns problems with attention. Attention and memory deficits are often thought to be interrelated. After all, a child needs to be able to pay attention to something before he can remember it. Think of the simple act of repeating a series of numbers or letters spoken by another. If a child is not able to repeat back as many numbers or letters as would be expected for her age, is it because she has a poor memory or because she wasn't paying attention? We often can't say for sure.

Children who have deficits in attention may demonstrate several of the following characteristics to a far greater extent than others of the same age:

- Difficulty maintaining focus on any one thing for more than a very short period of time

- Appearing absentminded or forgetful
- Appearing to become distracted when spoken to
- Being easily diverted from interests
- Difficulty completing assignments and following directions
- Losing things frequently
- Poor organization skills

Some, but not all, children with attentional problems may eventually be diagnosed with Attention Deficit/Hyperactivity Disorder (ADHD). Characteristics of this disorder often include deficits in attention and problems with hyperactivity and impulsivity; however, some children show symptoms only in one or two of these areas.

- Those who show problems in both attention and hyperactivity/impulsivity may be diagnosed as Attention Deficit/Hyperactivity Disorder, Combined Type.
- Those who show symptoms mostly in attention may be diagnosed as Attention Deficit/Hyperactivity Disorder, Predominantly Inattentive Type.
- And those who show symptoms mostly in hyperactivity and impulsivity may be diagnosed as Attention Deficit/Hyperactivity Disorder, Predominantly Hyperactive-Impulsive Type.

No one knows for sure what causes ADHD, but many believe it has to do with an imbalance of a certain type of brain chemical - or neurotransmitter - that impairs the child's arousal level and ability to focus and sustain attention. Many children with a diagnosis of ADHD can be helped tremendously through counseling, biofeedback training, behavior modification strategies, and perhaps medication that corrects the underlying chemical imbalance and allows them to better concentrate and focus their thoughts and attention. For some of these children, the difference such interventions make can be quite dramatic. Used to failure and repeated reprimands due to their constant activity and lack of focus, their self esteem and attitude toward school improves along with their ability to control their behavior and focus their attention.

Beware! Many experts believe that ADHD is often over-diagnosed or misdiagnosed. Characteristics of ADHD may be shown by many normally developing children and can also be confused with symptoms of other conditions, such as depression, anxiety, minor seizure disorder, or even giftedness. In fact, distinguishing between giftedness and ADHD is often very difficult to do. Gifted children can appear distracted, inattentive, impulsive, and hyperactive, too - as a result of boredom related to a mismatch between their intellectual needs and learning environment, or due to their need for an abundance of stimulation. While children can certainly both be gifted and have ADHD, it pays to be cautious when considering a diagnosis. It's not necessary - and it may be potentially harmful - to treat a child with medication for a neurochemical imbalance when providing a more challenging or meaningful curriculum might solve the problem instead. Keep in mind that it's often best to consider the simplest, least "pathological" explanation for a child's behavior first, before moving on to a medical diagnosis. For this reason, parents of intellectually bright children should seek the advice of someone familiar with both giftedness and ADHD when considering a treatment plan for their own children.

It's important to note here that there are many children with a diagnosis of ADHD who will not qualify for special education services under a learning disability condition when the discrepancy model is used. This is because many of these kids do not show a significant discrepancy between their ability (often measured through an IQ score) and their school achievement. They have been able to do well in school and work up to their potential despite their problems in attention.

Visual Processing

Children with visual *acuity* problems have difficulty seeing clearly. These children can often be helped through the use of prescription glasses or contact lenses. However, children with visual *processing* problems may have excellent acuity but have difficulty organizing, interpreting, or deriving meaning from what they see. For these types of visual problems, there is no easy fix.

People often associate the term "dyslexia" with a reading disorder related to a particular type of visual processing problem called *strephosymbolia* - a term coined by the late neurologist Samuel Orton in the 1930's to describe a condition where children confuse or reverse similar-appearing letters such as *b* and *d*, *p* and *q*, or *m* and *w*. These children may also reverse the order of letters in words they read (for example, confusing *was* for *saw*, or *brag* for *garb*) and make reversal mistakes with numbers (like seeing 87 as 78, or saying 16 rather than 61).

Such reversals and word confusions are common in younger children, simply because of developmental immaturity of the perceptual centers in the brain. However, in my experience, these symptoms are rare in those over the age of seven or eight. Rather, visual processing deficits are more likely to be associated with the following areas which directly affect a child's ability to read, write, solve math problems, and perform just about any other academic task.

Visual memory: The ability to remember what is seen. Children with a strong visual memory system only need to look at something once or twice for it to be imprinted in their minds. Those with problems in this area have difficulty holding what they see in mind long enough to process the information and get it into longer-term memory.

Visual discrimination: The ability to notice slight differences in similar-appearing objects, letters, shapes and numbers. Children weak in this area may have trouble identifying letters that have similar shapes, such as *h* and *n*, or G and C.

Object constancy: Recognizing shapes, numbers, and letters, even though they may be bigger, smaller, upside down, or somehow oriented differently in space. This ability allows a child to recognize the letter *z*, or the word *house*, for example, regardless of the size or type of font used, or whether the book is help right side up or upside down.

Visual figure ground: Being able to separate out and recognize symbols, shapes, letters, or numbers from background objects - for example, recognizing words and letters on a piece of paper that also contains a lot of other visual information like pictures, lines, or other graphics.

Visual problem solving: The ability to use mental or visual images to reason, understand concepts, analyze patterns, or compare solutions. Visual problem-solving is sometimes called "picture thinking" and is associated with the intuitive, simultaneous type of thinking associated with "right brain" activities. The ability to quickly solve puzzles or put differently patterned blocks together to match a design are examples of IQ test tasks that tap into this skill. Children who have a weakness in this area may compensate by talking things out in their minds or under their breath when thinking through a problem or trying to remember something they've read or seen.

Visual motor integration: While the skills discussed above mostly have to do with the way a child takes in and interprets visual information, visual motor integration deals more with output - the ability to integrate or coordinate what is seen and get it down on paper. Visual motor integration is sometimes called eye-hand coordination. Children with visual motor integration problems have a hard time with writing; their printing and cursive may appear sloppy or they may write slowly and laboriously.

"Is my child "dyslexic?" This is a common question heard by teachers and school psychologists. Dyslexia is an often-used term that many parents associate with a reading disorder caused by a visual perceptual problem in which a child reverses letters and words. For many educators, however, the term dyslexia has come to simply mean a learning disability in the area of reading. In the same way, dysgraphia means a learning disability in the area of writing, and dyscalculia means a learning disability in the area of math. Such learning disabilities may be caused by a visual perceptual problem, but they may also be the result of one or more of the other psychological process deficits reviewed in this chapter. As we've seen, whether a child can be said to have such a disability often depends on what definition or criteria are used in assessment.

Auditory Processing

Children with auditory processing deficits are those who, despite having normal hearing (or auditory acuity), have a hard time remembering, interpreting, or using what they hear.

Some areas of auditory processing include:

Auditory memory: The ability to remember what is heard. Children with this deficit will have difficulty remembering verbal directions or recalling elements of a story that is read to them. They will find it hard to hold what they hear in their minds long enough to use the information to solve problems or to understand concepts. These children will often need to have things repeated several times before they can finally understand or process the information they hear. Some children have difficulty remembering both numbers and words, while others seem to have trouble in only one of these areas. Other children may have difficulty remembering words in isolation but do quite well remembering whole sentences, since the words have been put into a meaningful context.

Auditory discrimination: The ability to recognize sounds and words and to perceive small differences between them. This skill also called "phonological awareness." Children with problems in this area may confuse or substitute similar-sounding words, or be unable to connect letters with sounds or sound combinations when learning to read.

Auditory reasoning: The ability to use words and language to reason and solve problems. Children with problems in this area may have difficulty answering comprehension questions or solving verbally presented word problems. They may also have difficulty following verbal directions from a parent or teacher, particularly when the directions involve multiple steps like, "Go to your room, pick up the clothes on the floor, put them in the hamper, and put the hamper next to the washing machine."

Language Deficits

Related to auditory processing deficits, language deficits involve problems with understanding and using speech. Language deficits are often divided into two general areas:

Receptive language: Even though they may have adequate auditory memory and auditory discrimination skills, children with receptive language problems have trouble understanding or using what they hear, and may find it difficult to follow complicated directions. They will also have a weak vocabulary, since they have difficulty connecting words with concepts or ideas.

Expressive language: Children with expressive language problems may understand what they hear (have good receptive language ability) but have problems retelling a story, or using complex and grammatically correct sentences. These children also have difficulty giving oral presentations and relating what they know to other people. Because of this, they may mistakenly be thought to have poor comprehension. Stuttering and problems with articulation (such as lisping) are also considered to be expressive language problems.

Ruling Out Other Reasons for the Learning Problem

Once a significant discrepancy between ability and achievement has been determined and a psychological process deficit has been found, the school's evaluation team still needs to establish that the learning problem has not in fact been caused by some other reason that has nothing to do with a learning disability.

Some other potential causes of school problems that need to be ruled out include:

- The child has not been attending school regularly and therefore has not had the opportunity to learn. We wouldn't expect a student who has missed several months of school because of family circumstances or a health issue to be doing grade-level work. A history of truancy or frequent moves may also affect a child's ability to learn.

- The student has an untreated vision or hearing problem which may have contributed to his poor school performance. A child who can't hear well or see the board because he has not been provided with (or refuses to wear) glasses or hearing aids will likely miss a lot of the instruction going on in the classroom.

- The tests used during the assessment were not valid given the student's background. For example, a student who doesn't speak English as a primary language or who has been attending school in a non-English-speaking country would not be expected to do well on an academic test of reading and writing given in English.

- The academic delays can be better explained by other conditions such as a language processing problem, a severe emotional disturbance, or a health condition that may cause tiredness and impact the ability to concentrate. Such students may qualify for special education services under other eligibility categories, even though they may not meet the district's criteria for a learning disability.

School psychologists often use a review of records, parent interviews, a look at health history (including vision and hearing checks), and sometimes clinical judgment when considering the impact these other factors may have had on a child's academic achievement scores.

The IEP Team Meeting

Once a child has been tested, the parent is invited to a meeting to review the results. If you are attending one of these meetings, don't be afraid to ask questions and offer your opinion. Remember, you are part - maybe the most important part - of the assessment team. Feel confidant that, having read this chapter, you're likely going to know more than most other parents who have come to the table.

If your child does not qualify for special education services, additional recommendations or suggestions may be made by the team members to help your child outside of the special education program. And keep in mind that, if your child continues to have learning problems in school, you can always request additional testing in the future. Some children who do not qualify for special education one year may qualify the next - so keep the option open.

If your child is found eligible for special education services, an "Individual Education Plan" or "IEP" will be developed. The IEP is essentially a document that outlines what services the student will receive. The IEP also includes test scores and other information on how the child is currently doing in school, and outlines academic goals that the child will work on over the next year.

A child's ongoing needs and progress are reviewed formally at least yearly at an annual IEP Team meeting. Also, every three years special education students are reevaluated to further assess their progress and to determine whether they are still eligible for services. Some show enough improvement to be exited from special education altogether, or at least to begin a gradual transition back to general education.

Children who qualify for special education services receive

support from teachers or specialists who are specifically certified in a particular area or program. I'll go over some basic types of services next.

Resource Specialist Program (RSP)

Placement in a resource specialist program (RSP) is often the first level of support offered to students who have been found to have a learning disability. Most of the children who receive RSP services have at least average cognitive ability - and many test in the above average, or even gifted, range. RSP students spend most of their day in a general education classroom and receive part-time support through the resource program in their areas of need. The type and amount of service will be determined by the IEP Team and will be specified on the IEP document.

The three basic kinds of RSP support are:

Pull-out or direct service. At the elementary level, students are removed from their general education classroom for subjects where they need extra support, and are taught in an individual or small-group setting in the resource specialist's room. At the secondary level, resource students may go to a resource classroom during one or more periods a day for a "study skills" program where they are given extra help in their area of need, or they may go to a resource room for one or more core subjects, like math or language arts, in place of taking these classes in the general education program.

Team teaching or collaboration model. The resource teacher goes into a general education classroom and works along side the general education teacher to support groups of students who need more individual attention. The resource teacher may work both with identified RSP students and with others in the class who need more individualized attention.

Consultation or "watch and consult." The student does not regularly receive any direct support from the resource teacher; instead the resource teacher helps the general education teacher modify or adapt the curriculum in the student's regular classroom or is available to support the resource student and general education teacher as needed - perhaps to review for a test or when there is a special long-term project.

The way the RSP program is set up at a particular school is often based on the needs of the students at that site. Some resource teachers use all three models in their program, and some use just one or two. Resource teachers typically have caseloads of 25 to 30 children and are qualified to teach and support students with many different types of disabilities, not just children with learning disabilities.

Special Day Class (SDC)

The special day class (SDC) provides a more intense level of service and is used for students who cannot make meaningful progress in the general education classroom, even with support from an RSP teacher. As the name implies, children who are placed in an SDC spend most of their day in a special education classroom with a teacher who is specifically credentialed to teach in that setting. These classes are ideally limited to about ten to twelve students and there is often an instructional assistant in the class in addition to the teacher giving more opportunity for individualized support and instruction. Some students may be integrated, or "mainstreamed," back into a general education classroom for part of the day for nonacademic areas or for subjects where they don't require as much support.

In the past, districts often had separate SDC programs for students with specific types of disability. For example, SDCs which served only those students who were classified as learning-disabled, others for those with speech or language impairments, and still others for students diagnosed with an emotional disturbance. Although some districts still run these types of programs for specific groups of students, such as those with autism or emotional disturbance, most now primarily use the "non-categorical" special day class model. That is, students are grouped together for instruction based on their learning needs, rather than on their disability label. Those with milder forms of disability, such as those with learning disabilities or language deficits who largely need academic remediation, are typically enrolled in a noncategorical mild/moderate special day class (M/M SDC). And those with more severe forms of disability who may benefit from a curriculum focused on basic life or functional skills may be enrolled in a noncategorical moderate/severe special day class (M/S SDC).

Related Services

Some children have special needs that can't be fully addressed in an RSP or an SDC setting. These students may receive services through another specialist - often called related services or "designated instructional services" (DIS) provider. These specialists frequently work with children in an individual or a small-group setting, and may travel from school to school to serve the students on their caseload. If a child receives these types of services, the related services provider will become part of the child's assessment team and will participate in the annual and three-year review IEP Team meetings.

Some of the more common related services include:

- Speech and language therapy
- Adaptive physical education

- Nursing services

- Counseling

- Physical therapy

- Assistive technology (the use of computers, language boards, or other devices to help students communicate or learn)

- Vision services (may include Braille instruction and providing students with large-print material or assistive technology)

- Audiological services (may include hearing checks, monitoring the use of hearing aides, and instruction in signing)

Least Restrictive Environment

In general, the more support a child needs, the more special education services he should be receiving. But keep in mind that, by law, districts are required to serve students in the "least restrictive environment," or "LRE." This is often interpreted as meaning that special education students must spend as much time with general education students as possible, while still receiving the services they need to support their progress. For this reason, when a child is initially tested and found to qualify for special education support under a learning disability condition, he will usually be placed in a resource specialist program rather than a special day class.   This way, he can remain in his general education classroom the majority of the day, while getting the services he needs on a part-time basis from the resource teacher. Children are only placed in a special day class when it is determined that they cannot make adequate progress even with maximum support from a resource teacher and from related services specialists. If a resource student continues to struggle academically, the IEP Team (which includes the parents) will often decide to increase the amount of RSP support the child is given before considering an SDC placement.

Some children receive a combination of special education program services, based on their learning needs. For instance, a child may spend part of her day in a general education classroom, part in a special day class, and part receiving support from a resource teacher. The same child might also receive help from an adaptive PE specialist for motor problems, or from a speech and language therapist to work on vocabulary skills. Flexible programming like this is sometimes called "blending."

Special education law is often complex, and there is some variation in the way states and individual districts run their programs. Special education terminology and acronyms can also vary from district to district. If your child is being tested, you should be given a copy of the current special education laws and parent rights pertaining to your state in language that you can understand. Look this information over carefully and don't be afraid to ask questions. Your most basic right is that you have input into any decision that is made regarding your child's education. You are considered an important member of the school team, not just an observer. The assessment team needs your input in order to do a thorough evaluation and be a better advocate for your child. For a more complete review of special education law and services in your state, go to your State Department of Education web site and follow the links to the area dealing with special education - or do a web search using the search terms "special education law" and the name of your state.

"Twice Exceptional"

If otherwise bright children can be learning disabled then what about those who are considered gifted? Can they be learning disabled too? Many experts agree that it is not only possible but relatively common.

As we've seen with the discrepancy model, learning-disabled children are often defined as otherwise capable students who are not working up to their potential in some area because of an underlying processing problem. These are children who show strengths in some areas and noticeable weaknesses in others. Many gifted children fit this pattern. An individual IQ test, the kind commonly used to diagnose giftedness in schools, is made up of several separate subtests measuring different areas like memory, visual spatial skills, and verbal ability. While a child's full scale, or overall, IQ score may fall in the gifted range, the pattern of scores on these individual subtests can vary widely. For example, some children show unusual strength in subtests which measure visual reasoning ability and a relative weakness in those measuring verbal areas. Other children show quite different patterns. In fact, rather than being universally gifted, most children with high IQs show a definite pattern of strengths and weaknesses, or peaks and valleys, when it comes to their cognitive abilities.

Similarly, gifted children can vary greatly in how well they do in school, depending on the subject area being considered. While they shine in some academic areas, they may struggle in others. Some of these children will be able to compensate, using their underlying strengths to make up for their weaknesses. But sometimes the process deficit - memory, attention, expressive language, or some other problem - is so severe that the child is not able to compensate. Children like these are sometimes called "twice exceptional," or "2E" kids.

Some of these children may eventually be tested for a learning disability by the school district and receive services through a special education program, in addition to whatever services they might be receiving from the district's gifted program. For example, a gifted child may be enrolled in a self-contained class for gifted students, and be pulled out two or three times a week by a resource specialist teacher for individualized instruction in reading, writing, or math. Another child may be enrolled in a cluster group with other gifted kids for instruction in her areas of strength - math or science, for example - and then, at other times, work within her general education classroom with a cluster group of resource students on her area of weakness.

Still, there are many gifted children out there who could benefit from help from special education services, but who are never identified for such services. There may be several reasons for this. For example, some districts do not use the discrepancy model to identify learning-disabled children. Rather than attempting to measure a child's "potential" with an IQ test and looking for children whose academic scores do not measure up, some districts use different criteria. They may qualify only those children who are working a certain number of grade levels below their grade placement in one or more subject areas - a fifth grader who is working at a second-grade level in reading, for instance. In these districts, gifted children are unlikely to be identified as learning disabled because, while they may be working far below their own IQ levels in certain school subjects, they are not likely to be working far below grade level.

Even in districts where the discrepancy model is used, many bright or gifted children may never be referred for testing for a learning disability. Parents of these children may not request testing because they believe that special education services are only for students with severe cognitive or physical disabilities. They are unaware that a child can be both gifted and learning disabled. Parents may also be afraid of labeling their child. Many are understandably hesitant to saddle their child with a term like "learning disabled," believing that this may damage the child's self-esteem or cause teachers to treat them differently, possibly lowering their expectations. And sometimes twice-exceptional children are never tested because their educational needs are already being met through creative scheduling or other programs on campus, so parents and teachers see no need to consider special education options.

For example, a second-grade gifted child who is working several years above grade level in math, but only at or around grade level in reading and writing because of an auditory processing deficit, may spend part of her day in a fifth grade classroom for math instruction alongside older students, and the rest of the day with her grade peers for instruction in reading, writing, and other areas with a skilled general-education teacher.

Others may receive support in their area of weakness through a general education remedial program on campus or through informal support from a resource specialist teacher. As you've read, some schools allow children who are not formally identified as special education students to receive help from the school's resource teacher. These programs are often called school-based programs, situational placements, resource collaboration programs, or informal placement programs.

Some twice-exceptional children may also be fortunate enough to be enrolled in a general education classroom with a teacher who has access to specialized instructional material and who is proficient at differentiating instruction (grouping children and challenging and supporting them at their own learning level) within the general education setting. Keep in mind that many general education teachers are trained at using the same type of approaches, curricula, and materials that special-education teachers use. A child does not necessarily need to be formally identified as learning disabled and served through a special education program in order to have access to the most highly trained teachers and the best instructional materials available in the district. When looking for the right educational program for a twice exceptional child, it usually comes down to finding the most competent, caring, and well-supported teacher the district has to offer. If you believe you have a "twice exceptional" child, work with your child's teacher, school psychologist, and school team to come up with flexible, creative options that fit your child's unique needs.

Are Learning Disabilities Permanent?

Many learning disabilities do turn out to be lifelong challenges. A child with a poor short-term memory or with problems in attention may have the same traits as a college student, or as a working adult. These children may continue to struggle with learning new concepts, solving complex mental problems, or using language fluently throughout their lives.

However, others will appear to "outgrow" their learning problems. Something seems to change, and what once was a struggle starts to come more easily. I've seen this myself on many occasions. Children who are several years below grade level in reading, for example, may start to catch up and begin reading fluently by the time they reach adolescence. Children with a severe language disorder begin to speak and understand as well as their age peers. Sometimes the changes are dramatic - like a light was suddenly turned on - and sometimes more gradual and subtle.

Reasons for such improvements may differ from one child to the next. However, some possible explanations include:

- The child may have learned to better compensate for his disability - to use his strengths to make up for his weaknesses. Those with receptive language deficits or short-term auditory memory problems, for example, may have learned to use visualization strategies, or become skilled at note taking and other studying techniques that help them bypass their auditory weakness. Sometimes these compensation strategies are explicitly taught to the child by a knowledgeable teacher; other times, the child learns to compensate on his own, through a natural process of trial and error.

- The child's brain has matured or developed in such a way that whatever "circuits" weren't previously connected quite right have now come together and begin to work. Some children's development seems to progress at a continuous and predicable rate, while others develop in sudden starts and stops - like a car with a manual transmission being driven by a beginning driver's ed student. It is also true that some children's neural systems develop less uniformly than others, with different areas of the brain blossoming at different times. These children may be very different from one year to the next, depending on how their brains have physically matured.

- The child has benefited from some special technique or curriculum that was not available earlier. For instance, some children learn better in classrooms where techniques like multi-sensory instruction or cooperative learning are emphasized. Similarly, some children will learn more efficiently with a phonics-based reading program, and others with a whole-language approach.

• The child never had a true learning disability in the first place. There is often a lot of subjectivity in determining who meets the criteria for a learning disability, and even though the evaluation team is supposed to rule out other reasons for a child's learning problem, this is often difficult - if not impossible - to do. Sometimes the "learning disability" is instead more the result of factors like poor school attendance or a lack of good instruction. Once the child is enrolled in a strong academic program and begins attending school regularly, his academic problems are quickly resolved. Children with learning problems may also show great improvement if what was thought to be a learning disability was actually an undiagnosed hearing or vision problem that is eventually corrected, or an underlying emotional problem caused by a situational stressor, such as a divorce, that is later resolved.

CHAPTER SEVEN

Bright Kids with Learning Problems

Quick Points

- Some difference in learning ability is normal. Most children have a definite set of strengths and weaknesses when it comes to how well they do in school.

- While some children can overcome their weaknesses by working harder or through compensating, others are not able to do so. These children may have a true learning disability - a persistent and obvious block when it comes to learning certain types of material.

- In most cases, there is no clear or observable cause for such problems. However, many experts believe that learning disabilities are caused by an underlying difference in the way the brain processes information.

- If your child is showing signs of a learning problem, meet with her teacher or with the school's intervention team to come up with possible solutions. Many schools have general education interventions in place that may help your child succeed.

- If general education interventions are not working, consider requesting that your child be assessed for special education services. Special education services are federally mandated programs to help children who need special support or instruction because of an underlying disability. The largest single category of students who receive these services are those who are identified as learning disabled. Most of these students score in at least the average range on an IQ test, and many score in the above-average, or even the gifted range.

- States and districts differ in how they identify students who qualify for special education services under a learning disability condition. One common method that often incorporates IQ testing is called the "significant discrepancy model." Here, a child's IQ score is compared to the child's scores on academic achievement tests. If the child's academic scores in one or more areas are much lower than would be predicted by the IQ test score, then a significant discrepancy between the scores is found to exist. A school psychologist then administers other tests to determine whether a "psychological process deficit" is present. Some common psychological process deficits involve memory, attention, visual processing, auditory processing, and language deficits. If the assessment team finds that the child's discrepancy is caused by a process deficit, then it may be determined that the child has a learning disability and qualifies for special education services.

The three basic types of special education services are:

> ❥ Resource Specialist Program (RSP). Children receiving services through an RSP program are still enrolled as full-time members of a general education classroom and receive part-time support from a resource teacher. These children may be pulled out of their general education class one or more times a week for instruction in the resource room, or the RSP teacher may go into the general education class to work with groups of students who need extra support.

> ❥ Special Day Class (SDC). Children in a special day class are not enrolled in a general education classroom. They need a more intense level of support, and

so they spend most of their day with a special education teacher, although they may be "mainstreamed" back into a general education class for nonacademic subjects or for subjects where they need less support.

➤ Related Services. Related services providers are specialists who work with students in specific areas of need that can't be fully met in an RSP or SDC setting. Types of related services support include speech and language therapy, adaptive physical education, nursing services, counseling, transportation, physical therapy, vision services, and audiological services.

• Children who receive special education services must be served in the *least restrictive environment*, or "LRE." This is often interpreted as meaning that special education students must spend as much time in the general education program as possible while still getting their needs met. For this reason, most children who are initially tested and found to have a learning disability will be offered services through a resource specialist program and perhaps through a related services provider, rather than being placed in a special day class. A special day class placement is usually made only when the child cannot make adequate progress even with RSP and related services support.

• Children who score in the gifted range on an IQ test can also be identified as learning disabled - particularly when the significant discrepancy model is used. Children who are identified as both gifted and learning disabled are sometimes called "twice exceptional." Some of these children get their needs met through flexible and creative programming in the general education setting, while others may receive formal support from a special education teacher.

160

- Many children with learning disabilities will continue to struggle with learning throughout their lives. However, some appear to "outgrow" their learning problems - perhaps since they have benefited from a certain instructional technique or learned to compensate for their weaknesses, or simply because their brains have physically matured in such a way that the underlying problem becomes less of an obstruction.

PART FOUR

IQ Testing and Intelligence
Background and Basics

CHAPTER EIGHT

IQ Testing in the Schools
How Did It Start?

"*A strange lady with a stopwatch made me play with puzzles and asked me weird questions.*" (Overheard comment of a seven-year-old girl telling her friend about her IQ testing experience)

Every day, a familiar scene is played out in thousands of schools across the country: an adult and a child who have never met before sit across a table from one another. After some good-natured attempts at encouragement, the adult asks the child to do such odd and seemingly unrelated tasks as put puzzle pieces together, define words, and copy unfamiliar shapes. Notes are taken, a friendly parting comment is made, and later a number which is supposed to reflect the child's learning ability is presented to a waiting parent.

Nothing unusual, right? Just a kid getting an IQ test. But stop and think, what's really going on here - and why is this happening? IQ testing has become so commonplace, so accepted as part of school culture, that very few of us ever stop to ask such questions.

You've read about how these tests are used in the schools to help determine which kids qualify for special programs. These next chapters are for parents who want a little more information - a deeper look into issues surrounding IQ testing and human ability.

The Evolution of the IQ Test

The idea that intelligence could be formally tested began in the late 1800s in England with Sir Francis Galton, a British scientist and cousin to Charles Darwin. Inspired by his cousin's discoveries about evolution and how traits in animals are passed down from one generation to the next, Galton became interested in the influence of heredity on human characteristics. Through his investigations, he became convinced that intelligence is largely inherited - passed down from one generation to the next in the same way as physical attributes such as hair color or height. In his book, Hereditary Genius (1869), he supported this idea by tracing the lineage of accomplished men and showing that they often came from prominent and well-respected families.

Of course, we now know that such "research" really can't tell us much. After all, the reason that these accomplished men came from accomplished families could very well have more to do with the money, power, and connections they were born into than with an inherited mental superiority. Still, the idea that intelligence and other traits were inherited became well-accepted and eventually gave support to the eugenics movement - the idea that society could be improved through the selective breeding of superior individuals. Galton, and others interested in eugenics, even went so far as to suggest restrictions on parenting to limit the breeding of the "feebleminded." Some proposed using mental tests to objectively sort people into desirable and less desirable groups for the purpose of such practices.

Although it's hard to imagine it now, the eugenics movement was enormously popular in both the U.S. and Europe in the early 1900s. Part of the plan was to create a society in which advantages would be given to people who "deserved" them, based on their intellect, rather than to those who were born into privileged families - an idea known as meritocracy. Eugenics was later rejected by most as an absurd and racist notion, particularly after the world witnessed the outcome of such thinking during World War II.

Early Tests - Senses and Movement

Throughout his career, Galton attempted to gather as much information as possible on human physical and mental characteristics so that he would have the information he needed to compare related and unrelated people, and to prove his theories. To this end, he ran a laboratory at the South Kensington Museum in London (now the Victoria and Albert Museum) where, for a fee, people could have themselves measured on tasks involving sensory or motor ability - largely how sensitive they were to differences in touch, sound, sight, smell and such traits as the ability to react quickly. Here, visitors filed by a long table and were rated on such things as their sensitivity to the smell of roses, their ability to sense small differences in weights placed in their hands, and their skill at distinguishing between the tints of different-colored wool.

These days, the notion that mental ability could be tested in such a way may seem bizarre. But, at the time, Galton and others believed that, because our knowledge of the world comes through our senses, those with superior sensory abilities would also have superior intelligence. Other researchers, both in Europe and in the United States, continued to use sensory discrimination tests and tests of coordination to study mental ability until it was later found that there was little relationship between performances on these measures and other signs of intelligence, like achievement in school. Although these early mental tests were later abandoned, Galton is credited with the first to attempt to objectively measure intelligence and his idea of creating a test of mental ability raged on.

Before the mental testing movement, *phrenologists* of the early 1800s believed that one could judge intellect, talents, and character by examining the shape of a person's head. "Bumps" on the skull were thought to result from the presence of underlying organs of the brain that represented psychological attributes. For example, a bump on the forehead was thought to reflect a tendency for kindness. Although phrenology has been discredited as a science, one of the basic ideas associated with the movement - that certain human abilities and talents are located in distinct areas of the brain - now appears to be true.

The First Practical Test

Alfred Binet, a French psychologist, is considered to be among the first to develop a test of intelligence that could be used to predict success in school. In the late 1800s, the French government asked Binet and his colleague, Theodore Simon, to come up with a way to group children by learning ability.

The request came about for very practical reasons. At the time, the French government was just beginning to require that all children attend school. Before this, most French students came from upper class families, since many children from the lower classes stayed home to work on the farm or as trade apprentices. With the introduction of required school attendance, a much more diverse group of children entered the classrooms, and teachers found it difficult to accommodate the wider range of abilities. The government was interested in finding a way to sort children who were intellectual capable from those who were not, in order to put the latter group into special schools and avoid the "disruption" they caused to the more capable students' education.

In developing their test, Binet and Simon reasoned that tasks involving areas like practical knowledge, problem solving, memory, and vocabulary would be better predictors of school performance than simple tests of the senses that Galton and others had used. To judge how well their tests worked, Binet asked teachers to rate their students on school achievement and found that those who scored higher on the mental tests were also those rated as high achievers by their teachers.

And there it was. For better or for worse, the first easy and quick way to sort students into learning groups was born. This work resulted in the 1905 Binet-Simon Scale - the grandfather of all contemporary intelligence tests.

The final scale involved 30 tasks of increasing complexity which included:

- Following simple commands
- Naming objects shown in a picture
- Explaining the differences between familiar objects
- Repeating sentences immediately after hearing them from the examiner
- Repeating numbers spoken by the examiner
- Identifying rhyming words
- Answering comprehension questions of increasing difficulty

The 1905 Binet-Simon scale is considered to be the first practical intelligence test, not only because of its power to predict school success but because it was relatively easy to administer and to score. Binet and Simon improved the test in 1908 by noting which items the majority of children at different ages could do correctly and then using this information to develop the concept of *mental age*. A child's mental age was determined by the highest set of items he could pass. For example, if a seven-year-old succeeded on items designed for a nine-year-old he was said to have a mental age of nine. Similarly, a seven-year-old who could only pass items appropriate for a five-year-old was said to have a mental age of five. The concept of mental age was simple to understand and an easy way to sort people by mental ability.

As interest in the idea of testing mental ability grew, Binet himself warned against using such tests to permanently label people or to promote the idea that a person's intelligence is a "fixed quantity" that cannot be increased. He believed that these tests should serve only as a way of identifying children who might benefit from extra help in school. His view was that intelligence could not be measured by a single score, and that mental tests should not be used to make a definitive statement about a child's ability. Binet also promoted the now well-accepted ideas that intelligence is influenced by both a person's experiences and their genetic heritage, and that mental skills could be enhanced through education and practical experiences.

Mental Testing Comes to America

The Binet-Simon test was never widely used in France. However, revisions of the test, including one developed by Henry Goddard, the Director of Research at the Vineland Training School (the first school in America dedicated to the education and study of persons with mental disability), became increasingly popular in the United States in the early 1900s. In 1908, Goddard traveled to Europe and brought back copies of the Binet-Simon scale which he translated, revised and began to use with the students at the Vineland School. Goddard's later revision of the Binet-Simon Scale became the most commonly used mental ability test in the United States for many years.

Unlike Binet, Goddard felt that intelligence was in fact a "fixed" trait and the result of a single underlying "function."

In his own words taken from the 1920 book, *Human Efficiency and Levels of Intelligence*, Goddard states:

"...our thesis is that the chief determiner of human conduct is a unitary mental process which we can call intelligence: that this process is conditioned by a nervous mechanism which is inborn: that the degree of efficiency to be attained by that nervous system and the consequent grade of intelligence or mental level for each individual is determined by the kinds of chromosomes that come together with the union of germ cells: that it is but little affected by any later influences except serious accidents as may destroy part of the mechanism."

The debate regarding whether intelligence is a fixed or changeable trait and whether all mental abilities can be attributed to a general underlying function continues to be one of the most discussed issues in psychological testing today. We'll take a look at these questions in the next couple of chapters.

IQ

Another American psychologist who revised the French Simon-Binet Scale was Lewis Terman of Stanford University. In his revision, Terman decided to use what he called an *intelligence quotient*, rather than a mental age when reporting the results of the test. A quotient is a number that results from dividing one number by another. To compute an intelligence quotient, or "IQ," Terman divided the child's mental age by her actual age and then multiplied the number by 100.

- For example, if a 5-year-old scored a mental age of 5, he would have an IQ of 100 (5/5 X 100 = 100)
- But if a 5-year-old scored a mental age of 6, he would have an IQ of 120 (6/5 X 100 = 120)
- And if a 12-year-old scored a mental age of 6, he would have an IQ of 50 (6/12 X 100 = 50)

As you can see, an average IQ was reflected in a score of 100 with lower mental ability being associated with scores lower than 100 and higher mental ability being associated with scores above 100. The same holds true today when interpreting modern IQ test scores.

The intelligence quotient was considered to be a better way to report scores on a mental test than simply reporting a child's mental age since it gives a better picture of how advanced or delayed a child is in relation to others. Suppose a ten-year-old earned a mental age of 12 on such a test. Using the concept of mental age we say she is two years ahead of "normal." Using the same idea, we could also say that a five-year-old who obtained a mental age of seven is two years ahead. Yet, the five-year-old should be considered more advanced, since two years is a bigger jump in ability in relation to her age.

By dividing mental age by chronological age, the IQ score reflects this fact.

- In this case, the ten-year-old would have an IQ of 120 (12/10 X 100) and the five-year-old would have an IQ of 140 (7/5 X 100)

Terman's 1916 adaptation of the Simon-Binet Scale was called the Stanford-Binet Intelligence Scale because of his association with Stanford University. An updated revision of this scale continues to be one of the most widely used IQ tests in the world.

The Point Scale

While the IQ had advantages over the mental age, there were still problems with its interpretation. One such problem was that the IQ formula often seriously underestimated the ability of adults. This is because intelligence, as measured on IQ tests, appears to level off in adolescence. Most adults are able to correctly answer about the same number of questions on an IQ test as someone in their late teens. So, in theory a 36-year-old adult who passed as many items as an average 18 year old could be assigned an IQ of only 50 (18/36 X 100 = 50), falsely indicating significantly below-average intelligence.

It's curious that, although IQ means "intelligence quotient," current intelligence test scores are not really quotients at all. A quotient is a number you get when you divide one number by another. While the original IQ formula involved dividing mental age by chronological age, thus obtaining a quotient, obtaining current IQ scores involves no such division. Yet by the time the original formula was abandoned, the term "IQ" had become part of our culture, forever associated with scores on intelligence tests.

For this reason, Robert Yerkes, an American psychologist, suggested replacing the traditional system of using mental age to calculate and report an intelligence score with what he called a point scale. Using the point scale, test takers are assigned points based on how well, and sometimes how quickly, they respond to test items as compared to others in their own age group. The higher the number of points received in comparison with the average number of points for others of the same age, the higher the IQ. In this way scores for those over eighteen more truly reflect their ability.

Group Testing

The biggest boost to intelligence testing came when the United States entered World War I in 1917. The government suddenly needed a more efficient way to screen and categorize a larger number of recruits than the time-consuming individually administered tests would allow. To solve this dilemma, a group of psychologists, including Robert Yerkes, the developer of the point scale, and Lewis Terman, coiner of the term "intelligence quotient," were asked to develop an easily administered group test.

Fortunately, Terman had a student named Arthur Otis who had already been working on a group-administered test. Much of the material in Otis's test was adopted by the psychologists. The final tests came to be known as the Army Alpha and Army Beta Tests. While both were designed to be administered to large groups of recruits at the same time, the Army Alpha Test was used more for routine testing, while the Army Beta Test was a nonverbal measure used with illiterate recruits or those who spoke a foreign language. The Beta Exam required recruits to do such things as complete mazes, solve puzzles, and identify visual patterns. Many nonverbal IQ tests used today contain similar tasks.

Group tests not only allowed large numbers of people to be tested for a very low cost, but also simplified the process of administration, meaning that intelligence testing could be done by someone with minimal training rather than a specialist such as a psychologist. For these reasons revisions of the Army Alpha and Army Beta Tests, as well as many other more recently developed group-administered tests, are still widely used today.

Looking Ahead

Over the last several decades hundreds of new IQ tests have been developed while well-established tests - such as the Stanford-Binet and the Wechsler Intelligence Scale for Children - are periodically refined. IQ testing of some kind has become common in many parts of society and is especially pervasive in our schools. Why? In part, because it's a fast and efficient way to sort students into different programs and to predict performance in school. Standardized achievement tests and college entrance exams are prevalent for much the same reasons.

IQ tests will probably be around for a while. But do these tests really measure intelligence? The quick answer is no, at least not all aspects of intelligence. But before that question can really be answered the term "intelligence" has to be defined - not an easy task. In the next two chapters we'll look at how some have attempted to do this and we'll consider the question of nature versus nurture when it comes to mental abilities.

CHAPTER EIGHT

IQ Testing in the Schools

Quick Points

- The idea that intelligence could be formally measured began in the late 1800s with Sir Francis Galton who believed that human traits were largely inherited. Galton believed that, since people gather information through their senses, the most "superior" of us would have the keenest senses. His early tests focused on examining a person's sensitivity to things like touch, sound, and light. Such tests were abandoned when it was found that performance on these measures had no relationship to other indicators of intelligence, such as achievement in school.

- Alfred Binet, a French psychologist, was among the first to develop a test that predicted school performance. His test involved such things as practical knowledge, reasoning, memory, and vocabulary - areas still measured through many modern IQ tests.

- Binet's test was never widely used in France. However, it was later translated, adapted, and revised by American psychologists, including Henry Goddard and Lewis Terman, and became one of the most widely used tests of intelligence in the world.

- Performance on tests of mental ability was originally reported using the concept of "mental age." A child's mental age was determined by the number of items she could pass. For example, a six-year-old who could pass test items designed for an eight-year-old was said to have a mental age of 8.

- The use of mental age was later replaced by the "intelligence quotient," or "IQ," which was derived by dividing a child's mental age by his chronological age, and then multiplying the result by 100.

- Because the original IQ formula was found to have some technical problems, including the tendency to underestimate the intelligence of adults, it was eventually replaced by the use of the point scale which derives a person's IQ by a comparison of their performance with the performance of others in the same age group.

- IQ tests continue to be used throughout society and are particularly prevalent in the school system.

CHAPTER NINE

What is Intelligence?

And Can It Really Be Measured?

Intelligence is a word that most of us think we understand - until we try to define it. Psychologists interested in measuring intelligence face the same dilemma. Try this: before reading further, put this book down and come up with a definition of intelligence on your own.

The definition you just created is as true as any other, including those of the supposed experts. This is because there is no general agreement as to how to define the psychological *construct* of intelligence. A construct is an abstract or general idea invented to describe a part of human behavior that can't be directly observed. Because you can't "see" intelligence, it cannot be objectively defined. It can only be inferred by observing a person's behavior. But what behavior should we be looking for? The answer will depend on just who you ask.

One reason why a definition is so hard to pin down is that views regarding intelligence are greatly influenced by cultural and family values. For example, in cultures where spiritual enlightenment is esteemed, intelligence might be defined as the ability to reach higher levels of spiritual awareness. In societies where hunting skills are important for survival, someone with good eye-hand coordination or a keen awareness of animal behavior would be considered smart. On the other hand, a computer whiz or an

English professor who depends on fast-food restaurants for nourishment might be judged as quite unintelligent in such a society.

In Western culture, definitions of intelligence are similarly influenced by social values. Rather than spiritual or physical skills, current Western definitions tend to involve traits having to do with cognition and higher order thinking. While there is considerable debate regarding what specific traits should be included, the following general attributes seem to be prevalent:

- The ability to think abstractly (to compare and contrast ideas; to apply existing knowledge to new situations)
- The ability to solve problems (to use information to find solutions and make rational decisions)
- The ability to understand and use language (to use verbal information to understand the world and express our ideas to others)
- The ability to learn (to understand and store information, and to use this information to support future learning)

To "g" Or Not To "g"

An ongoing debate regarding the definition of intelligence is whether there is a general power underlying all mental skills or whether it is better to think of the intellect as being made up of several different and relatively separate abilities.

Most would agree that there are those who appear to be gifted in certain areas of life while struggling in others. I know people who seem to have an inborn talent for drawing, painting, or other creative arts but are hopeless when it comes to anything having to do with math. There are others who excel in technology and computers, yet have a hard time communicating with or relating to other people.

Despite these apparent individual differences, some suggest that all human abilities are the result of a single underlying trait known as *general intelligence,* or "*g.*" Many psychologists support this idea by using the statistical techniques of correlation and factor analysis to show that those who score high in one area of mental ability tend to score high in others. For instance, those who do well on tests of memory are likely to do well on tests of vocabulary and comprehension.

Charles Spearman, a British psychologist, was an early advocate of this idea. He claimed that all abilities were somehow related to g, which he described as a "general mental energy." Spearman believed that g was best described as the ability to perform complex tasks that involved higher-level thinking skills like reasoning, comprehension, and the ability to compare and contrast ideas. He believed that less complex skills often measured on intelligence tests - such as memory, writing speed, and calculation of numbers - were strongly influenced by these higher order thinking skills. In other words, a person strong in g is likely to have strong skills in these less complex areas and, conversely, someone low in g is likely to display relatively weaker skills. Spearman called this idea the *"two-factor theory of intelligence."*

Spearman's Two-Factor Theory of Intelligence

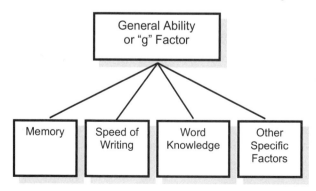

Although Spearman's concept of g has been widely researched and supported by many psychologists, there are others just as convinced that this model is wrong. As noted before, Spearman used a statistical method called factor analysis in arriving at his conclusions. Yet, there are many different forms of factor analysis and many different ways one can interpret the results.

In 1938, an American psychologist, Louis Thurstone, used results from another type of factor analysis to dispute the existence of g, and suggested that intelligence is really composed of a set of seven primary mental abilities that are relatively unrelated to one another. In other words, he proposed the idea that people can be advanced in some abilities without being advanced in others. Other researchers used statistical analysis to break down mental ability into even larger sets of independent factors.

Fluid and Crystallized Abilities

In the 1960s, two American psychologists, Raymond Cattell and John Horn, came up with a new way of looking at things. These researchers used statistical techniques to categorize human ability into two types of aptitudes which they called *fluid* and *crystallized intelligence*.

Fluid intelligence is more associated with innate ability and what most people associate with the concept of "being smart." This type of intelligence can be described as an inborn capacity to think complexly and grasp new ideas. Speed of reasoning and memory are also associated with fluid intelligence. Cattell and Horn found that fluid intelligence generally increases until young adulthood, then plateaus before it gradually begins to decline due to the aging process; supporting the observation that many artists appear to do their most creative work during the first half of life.

Crystallized intelligence, on the other hand, refers to the

knowledge and skills that one acquires through learning and experience. This type of intelligence is related to achievement. Tests of vocabulary, general information, or math calculation skills assess crystallized intelligence. Unlike fluid intelligence, a person's store of crystallized intelligence can increase indefinitely throughout his or her life through the accumulation of new experiences. For instance, our vocabulary can continue to increase as we age if we continue to expand on the types of material that we read.

Cattell and Horn proposed that the development of crystallized intelligence is influenced by the strength of a person's fluid intelligence. That is, we are inclined to acquire more knowledge if we are endowed with a higher capacity to think complexly. As a result, crystallized and fluid abilities are highly correlated.

Some researchers believe that the concept of fluid and crystallized intelligence is really a refinement of Spearman's two-factor theory of intelligence, rather than a completely novel idea. However, the model has had quite an impact, and many researchers today use the notion of fluid and crystallized abilities when discussing intelligence.

Practical Intelligence

American psychologist Robert Sternberg was one of the first to suggest that there is more to intelligence than that which can be measured on a test. Sternberg reportedly became interested in questions related to IQ testing as an elementary school student when he was mistakenly labeled as a slow learner due to test anxiety. For several years school officials, noting his poor performance on an IQ test, expected little of him. He credits one particular teacher who ignored the test results and gave him extra support for helping him on his path to high achievement.

Out of this experience, Sternberg realized that IQ tests are often unreliable predictors of success in life and that people who do well on these tests are not necessarily those who are able to apply their knowledge to real-world situations. To address this matter, Sternberg developed the *triarchic theory of intelligence.*

This theory proposes that intelligence is really made up of three components.

- Analytic intelligence which is most closely related to traditional ideas about ability and is primarily associated with academic problem-solving skills.

- Creative intelligence which deals with the ability to use past experience to deal with new situations. Someone who is able to apply his or her current job skills to a different career path is demonstrating this aptitude.

- And practical intelligence which involves the ability to deal successfully with everyday tasks and to direct abilities toward meaningful goals. People who are able to understand their own strengths and weaknesses and apply this knowledge toward achieving their goals would be using this intelligence.

Perhaps the most significant aspect of Steinberg's theory is the notion that the definition of intelligence should include a consideration of how we perform in the everyday world - that is, after all, what IQ tests are supposed to predict.

The Theory of Multiple Intelligences

Howard Gardner, an American psychologist from Harvard University, proposed another nontraditional theory regarding how to view human intelligence. He noted that traditional IQ tests measure mostly logical reasoning and verbal skills, but don't tell us anything about other genuinely useful human abilities. He pointed out that many talented and successful people who demonstrate high levels of success in life, and who may even be considered brilliant by others, do poorly on IQ tests. Similarly, there are people who score very well on IQ tests, but seem unable to apply their abilities to any productive or meaningful use.

In his 1983 book, *Frames of Mind*, Gardner proposed his *theory of multiple intelligences* which suggested that intelligence is more than a general trait that can be measured on an IQ test. Gardner, instead, proposed that we have multiple "intelligences" that result from relatively independent systems in the brain.

In creating his theory, Gardner was interested in finding those abilities, or intelligences, that were valued across cultures. Rather than simply looking at test scores to locate these abilities, he drew on information from such disciplines as biology, psychology, neurology, sociology, and the arts.

One criterion for inclusion on the list of intelligences included the potential of isolation by brain damage. Gardner reasoned that if an area of human aptitude could be impaired by surgical or accidental damage to a specific area of the brain, then that area must represent a relatively independent ability. For example, it has been shown that through an incision in one specific area of the brain - in an operation designed to remove a tumor, for example - a person's ability to recognize a simple musical tune might be impaired. A lesion in another area of the brain may destroy a person's ability to speak or understand language.

Another criterion for inclusion on the list of intelligences was the existence of the trait in prodigies, savants, or other exceptional people. A prodigy is a person who appears naturally gifted and displays skills well beyond her years in areas such as math, art, music, or athletic ability. A savant is a person who has remarkable skills in one specific area, but is apparently delayed in others. A child with autism who appears to be socially and cognitively delayed but who is brilliant at playing the piano or manipulating numbers would be considered a savant. Gardner reasoned that the demonstration of such highly uneven skills further supported the idea that these traits were largely independent intelligences.

The idea that an intelligence must be genuinely useful and important, and result in an "end state" performance, talent, or profession, was also used as a selection criterion. An end state can be seen in individuals who are particularly competent in one or more of the intelligences, as may be reflected by the mastery of a certain job or avocation. For instance, a person who is exceptionally skilled in verbal areas may become a talented poet. Similarly, mathematical intelligence can be seen in the end state of an accomplished mathematician or scientist.

Using these and other criteria, Gardner originally proposed the following seven intelligences, and suggested a person who embodied each one. The first two are the skills usually associated with school learning and those most often assessed on IQ tests. The next three are often associated with the arts, while the final two are what Gardner calls the "personal intelligences."

- Verbal intelligence involves understanding and using language (poet T.S. Eliot)
- Logical-math intelligence is associated with the ability to reason abstractly and to solve math problems and problems of logic (scientist Albert Einstein)
- Spatial intelligence deals with the ability to perceive and use visual information (artist Pablo Picasso)
- Musical intelligence involves the ability to appreciate, compose, and perform music (composer Igor Stravinsky)
- Bodily kinesthetic intelligence is the ability to express one-

self physically or athletically through sports or arts such as dance (dancer Martha Graham)

➤ Interpersonal intelligence is the ability to understand and relate to other people (psychiatrist Sigmund Freud)

➤ Intrapersonal intelligence involves self understanding and the ability to be in control of one's own inner nature (philosopher and leader Mahatma Gandhi)

Gardner believes that each of us possesses all of these intelligences and that they work together in complex ways. He also emphasizes that, while there is a genetic component to the intelligences, they can all be enhanced or improved through practice.

The theory of multiple intelligences gives us a language to rethink how we value each others' abilities and to broaden our concept of "giftedness." There are many gifted people in the world who would not be identified as such on an IQ test which measures only verbal and logical reasoning skills, but little else.

Who is more intelligent: A professional athlete or a famous singer with perfect pitch? A politician who understands how to motivate other people and gather their support or a talented painter? A mathematician or an accomplished novelist? These are ridiculous questions when you realize that the answer depends on how the term intelligence is being defined. All of us have gifts, or relative strengths, that can be recognized and honored.

While Gardner's theory has not been widely accepted in the academic community, the concept of multiple intelligences has been very popular with educators. This is probably because the idea validates what most teachers already know - that children have relative strengths and learn in different ways. These ideas make intuitive sense and provide useful information for those looking for ways to rethink teaching. Many teachers design lessons to include music, movement, art and other activities associated with the intelligences in order to connect with student strengths.

One of the major contributions of Gardner's theory is the recognition that social skills (interpersonal intelligence) and personal insight (interpersonal intelligence) are as valuable, if not more so, than the verbal and reasoning skills measured on traditional IQ tests. It's probably true that our personal happiness is more related to these skills than to any others. A number of theorists, including Daniel Goleman in his book, *"Emotional Intelligence,"* have since expanded on this idea.

Gardner's Original Multiple Intelligences with Sample "End States"

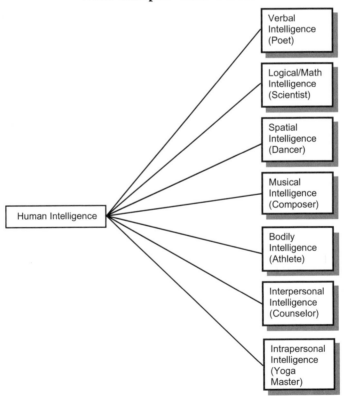

CHAPTER NINE

What is Intelligence?

Quick Points

- There is no single agreed-upon definition of intelligence. Because you can't "see" intelligence, it can't be objectively defined.

- Definitions of intelligence are influenced by cultural values - feelings about what skills and traits are important in a particular cultural setting.

- In Western culture, traditional definitions of intelligence often include the ability to think abstractly, to problem-solve, and to learn.

- One controversy regarding definition is whether to think of intelligence more as a general underlying "mental energy" or to regard it as being made up of several fairly independent parts.

- Charles Spearman, a British psychologist, believed that all mental abilities were related to this general underlying mental energy - which was later called "g."

- An American psychologist, Louis Thurstone, disputed the existence of g and claimed that intelligence was made up of seven primary unrelated abilities.

- In the 1960s Raymond Cattell and John Horn suggested that intelligence is really composed of two general types of abilities - fluid intelligence which involves the ability to think complexly and grasp new ideas, and crystallized intelligence which is associated with acquired knowledge.

- American psychologist Robert Sternberg suggested that the definition of intelligence should include the ability to apply what we know in practical everyday situations.

• Howard Gardner, an American psychologist associated with Harvard University, developed the theory of multiple intelligences. Gardner's view is that traditional IQ tests measure only a narrow band of human abilities and can seriously underestimate a person's true potential. Gardner proposed expanding our view of intelligence to include such abilities as spatial awareness, musical ability, athletic skill, interpersonal insight, and social skills, in addition to the verbal and math skills measured on traditional IQ tests.

Chapter Ten

Nature, Nurture, and Other Influences

Why We Are Who We Are

Are we the result of our biology or our experiences? Does your child get that personality quirk from you or did she learn it somewhere? Think about your own traits - your mannerisms, temperament, habits. Notice any similarities to your parents? Most of us do.

Early views on the *nature vs nurture* question tended to be extreme and one-sided. For example, in Europe in the 1700s there was a heated debate between the "nativists," who believed that all human traits were the result of genetics, and the "sensationalists," who felt that a person's intellect could be altered through experience.

The English philosopher, John Locke, a sensationalist and founder of the theory of empiricism, thought of the mind as a *tabula rasa*, a blank slate that can only be developed through learning and experiences. In this view, all children have infinite potential. Given the right environment and the right kind of experiences, any baby could blossom into a talented and accomplished adult.

In a now-famous experiment, a young French physician, Jean Itard, sought to prove this theory. In 1799, a young boy was found living in the woods near the town of Aveyron. The boy was naked and appeared to be afraid of human contact. The towns-people soon came to the mistaken conclusion that Victor, as the boy was later named, had been raised by wolves.

When Itard heard the story, he was intrigued. If Victor had been raised with no human contact, he was essentially a blank slate waiting to be shaped by the right experiences. Itard saw an opportunity to prove the sensationalists right by showing that he could teach Victor to become a "civilized" member of society.

It is now believed that Victor was a child with autism or some other form of mental disability who was abandoned by his parents. Victor's disability probably contributed to his inability to learn language. We also now know that there is a critical period in which certain skills can more easily be acquired. The critical period for language acquisition is in childhood - and Victor was just entering adolescence when he was found. See *feralchildren.com* for more information on Victor and other similar cases.

Yet after five years of daily lessons, Itard considered his experiment a failure. While Victor did learn how to take care of himself and lost his fear of people, he never learned to speak fluently or to read.

Extreme views regarding nature vs. nurture are now rarely heard. Current research suggests that human traits such as intelligence are the result of both of these influences. What we become is not solely due to one factor, but rather to a complex interplay between our genes and our surroundings. But just how much of measurable intelligence is due to genetics is still open to debate. Estimates range anywhere from twenty to eighty percent, with many experts settling on around fifty percent - or half.

We do not inherit our intelligence. Rather, we inherit a set of genes that may set limits on our potential. Genes may predispose us to develop in a certain way or to learn certain things more easily than others, but what we ultimately become is the result of the interplay between our genetics and our experiences. Researchers use the words *genotype* and *phenotype* to describe this phenomenon. Genotype describes the set of genes we are born with while phenotype describes what we become through our interaction with the environment. Two people with the same genotype (identical twins) may very well end up with different phenotypes - different personality quirks, different likes and dislikes, different talents - based on environmental influences.

So both genes and environment play a role in determining why we are who we are. But that's not the whole story. To get a better picture of the nature - nurture interplay we also need to take into account how each individual responds to environmental experiences.

Consider two children who are genetically programmed to be "average" in artistic ability. Given no special training or enrichment activities in painting, both would likely be average painters. But provide both with an "enriched" environment, which includes an abundant supply of art materials and frequent art lessons, and one of these children becomes an expert painter while the other shows little improvement.

What happened? Both children were destined by their genes to be average painters, but just one blossomed in an art-rich environment.

While we are all different in our genetic makeup, we are also different in the degree to which our genetic destiny can be altered through experiences. Researchers call this concept *plasticity*. Plastic can be easily altered, shaped, and molded, given the right environment (heat, for instance). Similarly, while all children can develop their inborn abilities to some extent, some are more readily shaped and molded by their experiences than others.

Yet another factor that complicates the question of how genes and environment interact is the concept of *reciprocal determinism*. We are not just passive sponges when it comes to our environment and experiences - we are active participants. Some of us may feel compelled to seek out certain activities that others actively try to avoid.

"He learned all about genetics at school today."

What Influences Ability?

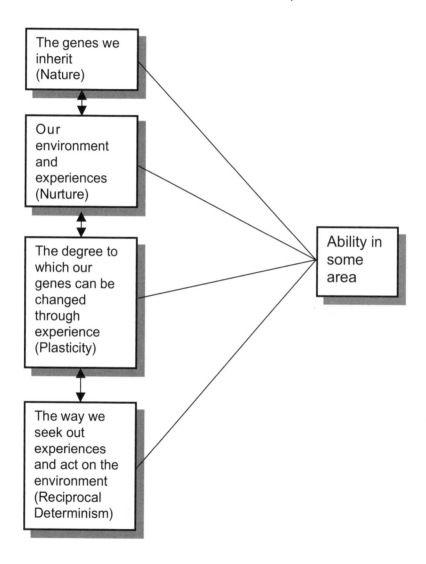

Put two children in the same preschool classroom and one may gravitate toward art activities while the other appears more interested in building blocks. Why? It may be that we seek out experiences that complement the part of our intellect that is more highly developed due either to inborn ability or to past experiences. It may also be that the child's interest in the particular activity was encouraged by a supportive adult, or by other children.

It appears that we are who we are not only due to the interplay between genes and environment, but also because of how we are compelled to act on the environment, and how susceptible we are to change as a result of our experiences.

Complicated, isn't it? The question of how heritable a trait is - any trait, including the ability to score well on an IQ test - can not be answered for any one person by looking at estimates of group averages. That answer is different for each individual.

Next, I'll review some research findings that can help us understand this complex interplay between biology and experience.

> While genetics do have an influence on the skills measured on IQ tests, a child of parents with unusually high or low IQs will tend to score more toward the average range. Researchers call this phenomenon "regression toward the mean." For instance, a child born to parents with IQs around 130 (really high) may score somewhere between 100 (average) and 130 – high, but closer to average than the parents. The same thing seems to hold true for physical characteristics like weight and height.

Rats!

In the late 1950s, researchers selectively bred two groups of rats according to how "smart" they were in running through a maze. The smarter rats were those that made fewer mistakes and were able to get through the maze faster. When raised under similar conditions, the rats that were bred from the smart group did consistently better at running through mazes than those bred from the "not-so-smart" group. This seemed to confirm that rat smarts were highly heritable.

But wait! It was also found that when the smart rats were raised in a poor environment - in which they were provided no rat toys and nothing interesting to look at - they did just as poorly on the maze test as the not-so-smart rats. Further, the not-so-smart rats did just as well as the smart rats when they were provided with an enriched environment with brightly colored walls, exercise wheels, and such. These findings suggest that the rats' genetic disposition to be superior or inferior maze runners could be altered, in either direction, through environmental experiences.

Twins

To look at the question of genetic influence on development, researchers often study the IQs of those with different degrees of genetic connection: brothers and sisters, parents and children, and so on. Yet when it comes to testing the effect of genes over environment, the study of twins is of special interest.

Identical twins develop from one egg, so the genes they inherit are identical. Fraternal twins develop from different eggs and, like ordinary siblings, have only about half their genes in common.

Probably the best insight into the influence of genetics on IQ can be found in studies looking at identical twins raised in different homes. These twins share the exact same genes but are exposed to different environments. Since identical twins share the same genotype, any difference in IQ can be attributed to the different home situations. Findings from these studies show that indeed the IQ scores of identical twins raised in different homes are quite similar, although less so than identical twins raised together. Again, these results seem to confirm that there is both a genetic and an environmental influence on IQ.

Another finding of twin studies is that fraternal twins tend to be more similar in IQ than non-twin siblings, even though they share the same degree of genetic relationship. This finding again supports the notion of environmental influence. Because they are the exact same age, it is likely that fraternal twins will share more environmental experiences than non-twin siblings. For example, they may be placed in the same preschool program together, and be given roughly the same amount of attention by their teachers and parents.

One famous twin study was published in the early 1950s by Cyril Burt, a well-known British psychologist. Burt was one of the first to report that the IQs of identical twins raised apart were more closely related than those of fraternal twins. He concluded that genetic influences were much more important than environment. However, after his death, Burt's research was called into question and he was officially accused by other leading researchers of fabricating data to support the idea that intelligence is inherited. While other researchers have since validated Burt's findings, his research still remains controversial and is often excluded in reviews of twin-study research.

Adoption

Adoption studies have also been used to look at the interplay between genetics and environment. Since there is typically no genetic relationship, any unusual similarity between adopted children's IQ scores and those of their adoptive parents is likely due to the home environment.

Different researchers have drawn different conclusions regarding adoption studies, yet many agree on the following:

- There is some relationship between the adopted child's IQ and that of the adoptive parents and siblings - although the relationship is not as strong as for family members who are genetically linked.

- Adoptive families can have a substantial influence on an adoptive child's development, including that part of development that is measured on IQ tests.

- Children who are adopted from "poorer" environments into homes which provide a good deal of support and enrichment activities often show the most sizeable increase in IQ scores.

- After leaving their adoptive home, adopted children's IQs may gradually become more similar to that of their biological parents.

Birth-Order Advantage?

For years, there has been an ongoing debate about the effect of birth order on intelligence. Many studies appear to show that, on average, those born earlier in a family score better on IQ tests than those born later. The farther down the birth ladder, the lower the IQ is likely to be. Common environmental explanations for this finding include:

- As infants, firstborns do not have to share parental attention with siblings - and more attention means more intellectual stimulation.

- Firstborns are, for a time at least, only exposed to their parents' grown-up language. Later-born children live in a home where the language has become "diluted" by the less mature speech of their sibling(s).

- Firstborn children often explain things to their younger siblings, giving them more practice with verbal skills.

- Firstborns are likely to begin life in a family where there are relatively more financial resources. As the family grows, these resources are spread more thinly. There may not be as much money for books, educational programs, and other enrichment activities like family trips.

Most birth order studies only find a few IQ points difference between siblings of differing birth order and, like many research findings involving influences on IQ, the whole idea of the birth-order advantage is controversial. There are some researchers who believe that it doesn't exist at all.

One criticism focuses on the way that birth-order studies are conducted. Most studies select large groups of unrelated people and measure their IQs. They then compare the IQ scores of first-borns with later-born children in these groups and discover the trend - the later the child is born, the lower the IQ.

But this method has a major flaw. Rather than looking at the effect of birth order, the studies may be measuring the effect of family size. When these studies look at the IQs of all third-born children, for instance, they are looking at children who come from families with three or more children. When they consider the IQs of fifthborns, they are considering those who come from families of five or more children. However, firstborns come from families with only one or more children, so any observed effect on IQ may, in fact, be related to the number of children in the family, rather than to the order of birth.

To try to get at the truth behind the birth order question, some researchers have conducted a different type of study. Instead of looking at a "snapshot" of large groups of unrelated people as previous studies had done, they looked at the effect of birth order within individual families over time. This way they were able to avoid confusing birth order with family size.

The results? Most researchers using these methods have found absolutely no relationship between birth order and IQ. In the families studied, fourth-born children did as well as second-borns, firstborns did no better than fifthborns, and so forth.

Other researchers have further complicated the birth-order debate by reporting that later-borns actually appear to have some advantages over their earlier-born siblings. Some findings suggest that later-born children may in fact be more be creative than their firstborn siblings, and are more likely to becomes leaders and to excel in such fields as science.

So what's the final word? There are a lot of good reasons why you might choose to limit your family size, but birth-order advantage shouldn't be one of them. As a parent, you really don't need to worry that each new addition to your family is predestined to be outdone by their older siblings.

Finally, it must be kept in mind that most psychological studies are looking at average differences in large groups of children, not at individuals. And within these research groups, there are many children who do not perform like the average child performs. For example, in birth-order studies, there are bound to be many later-born children that score better on IQ tests than the firstborn in the family. Again, "average" differences say nothing about how an individual child will perform.

So Does Family Size Matter?

While birth order may not be significantly related to IQ, most experts agree that family size is. Study after study has shown that children from larger families tend to, on average, have slightly lower IQs than those from smaller families or single-child homes. Why? Probably for the same reasons that some thought firstborns would have an advantage. Children from smaller families get more attention, more adult stimulation and modeling, and they benefit from more family resources - money and time. The larger the family, the more thinly those resources are spread.

Again, the studies in this area only reported average differences among very large groups of children, and the differences were not that impressive, only a few IQ points in most cases. Clearly, there are many children with high IQs who come from large families, and the many positive benefits of living with a large group of siblings may well outweigh the benefits of providing more individualized attention to a smaller brood.

The Flynn Effect

One peculiar finding that seems to corroborate the importance of environmental influence on intelligence is that, in several countries where intelligence testing is prevalent, IQ scores have gone up steadily over the course of the past several decades. Researchers call this phenomenon the "Flynn Effect," after the New Zealand researcher, James Flynn, who discovered this pattern. Some research has shown an average increase in IQ of as much as 15 points (a significant amount) between the years 1940 and 1990 - or about three points per decade. There are many possible explanations, but no general agreement, as to why this is happening.

Some of the possible explanations include:

- Improvements in nutrition and health care have lead to improvement in brain development. Those suggesting this idea note that improvements in IQ correspond to increases in average height and weight over the same time period.
- The trend toward smaller families has allowed more resources to be directed at improving children's abilities.
- Greater availability of toys and games has helped children to improve their visual and spatial skills.
- Increased exposure to test-taking strategies due to the increased emphasis on test taking in schools and in the workplace.
- An increase in the amount of time children spend in school and improvements in educational programming.

As you can see, all of these proposed explanations are environmental in nature. It seems unlikely that humans have become genetically smarter through evolution in such a short period of time.

What About Gender Difference?

Boys and girls may have many noticeable differences when it comes to behavior patterns. For instance, during unstructured activity boys tend to play more aggressively, while girls may gravitate toward more verbal or social activities.

But what about differences in IQs? Most researchers believe that there is little to no difference in overall ability between boys and girls as measured by IQ tests. However, there does appear to be some slight differences in *patterns* of ability when looking at some very specific areas.

For example, some studies show that males tend to perform better than females on certain spatial tasks that involve mentally rotating a three-dimensional object, while females may do better on verbal tasks such as recalling specific words.

To explain why males and females may perform differently in such specific areas, some researchers look to the field of evolutionary biology, which concerns how human traits and behaviors may have been shaped over time through adaptations to environmental influences. For instance, it may be that males developed particular spatial abilities because they needed those skills for hunting and shaping weapons, while women developed certain verbal skills because of the importance of language in promoting group and family unity.

What are These Environmental Influences?

So it's agreed, genetics do not explain everything when it comes to the ability to perform well on an IQ test. Then what are some of these outside forces that shape our intellect? Below is a partial list of environmental factors that may contribute to the enhancement of intelligence.

- Good nutrition and medical care which leads to favorable conditions for optimal neurological development. It has been found, for example, that providing vitamin and mineral supplements to children with poor diets enhances nonverbal or fluid intelligence.

- Family background and home environment. Children's IQ scores appear to be enhanced when they live in homes where the parents are well-educated and which provide high-quality language modeling (parents use appropriate grammar, have a large vocabulary) and lots of enrichment activities.

- The presence of books and other educational material in the home.
- Good schooling and regular school attendance.
- The presence of an encouraging adult who helps the child explore new ideas and provides instruction in basic skills.

While all of the above conditions can be considered "environmental" influences, it is sometimes challenging to separate out genetic effects. To do so, researchers would need to understand the direction of the relationship between IQ and any supposed influences - the classic chicken and egg question.

Take the finding that IQ gains have been shown to be associated with access to books and learning. Is this because more access to books leads to a higher IQ or is it that children with higher IQs tend to come from more intellectual families who keep a lot of books around the house? Many conditions that appear related to the home environment may in fact be equally related to family background or genetics.

Researchers have also found a relationship between a child's IQ and that of her best friend. Interesting discovery, but what does it mean? Do the IQs of children rub off on one another, or do children who are similar intellectually seek each other out as companions? It's probably a little bit of both.

Does IQ Change Over Time?

If environment is so important, can a child's IQ score change significantly over time, as they gather new experiences? Yes, of course: I've seen this myself on many occasions. IQ scores obtained after the early elementary years tend to be pretty stable on average, but an individual child's IQ score can sometimes change dramatically - particularly when exposed to certain kinds of learning experiences between the administrations of the two tests.

For instance, many commonly used IQ tests include measures of verbal skills such as vocabulary or verbal comprehension. If a child is tested at an early age and at a time when, for whatever reason, she has not been exposed to higher-level language modeling, she may not do well on the verbal section of the IQ test which would suppress her overall IQ score. If, later, the child is immersed in a language-rich environment, perhaps through a change of living situation or enrollment in a good school program, she may do better on the verbal aspects of the test thus raising her overall IQ.

It should be noted that some skills measured on IQ tests are more resistant than others to improvement through experience or learning. These skills, associated with the concept of fluid intelligence as discussed in Chapter Nine, have less to do with school learning and more to do with general reasoning ability or problem solving. Solving an abstract visual puzzle or finding a path through a complicated maze are examples of tasks designed to measure this type of ability.

IQ may change for purely genetic reasons as well. While we can make assumptions about the average developmental stages most children go through, we can't use these assumptions to say for sure how an individual child will develop. A child's IQ may be somewhat different from one test to the next depending on which areas of the neurological system have recently blossomed.

Potential

We now know that both our genes and our environment influence our development. While genes may set limits on who we become, it is our experiences with the world which allow our true abilities to be actualized.

Each child's experience in the world is unique, complex, and ever changing. Children are born into a set of circumstances, yes, but they are also capable of actively seeking out, interpreting, and directing their own experiences.

A single score on an IQ test tells us only how a child performed on a particular test at a particular time, and says little about that individual child's true potential. Under the right conditions - good schooling, encouraging parents, and the opportunity to explore interests - a child's ability in any area can reach its full expression.

The importance of a caring and supportive adult to a child's development was revealed in a well-known study conducted by the researcher, Emmy Werner. Werner and her colleagues followed a large group of Hawaiian children from birth through adulthood and discovered that among those born into poor conditions there was a distinct group that overcame these obstacles and matured into healthy, high-functioning adults. It was found that an outgoing and positive disposition and the presence of a caring and supportive adult were among the factors that made the difference in these resilient children.

CHAPTER TEN

Nature, Nurture, and Other Influences

Quick Points

- It is well accepted that intelligence is influenced by both nature (our genetic heritage) and nurture (our experiences).

- We are born with a set of genes that may predispose us to develop in a certain way and also set limits on this development.

- Our interaction with the environment - our experiences - can enhance or suppress our genetic tendencies.

- Just as we all differ in our genetic makeup, we also differ in the degree to which our genetic destiny can be altered through experience.

- We are not passive sponges when it comes to environmental influences - we are active participants. We tend to seek out experiences that interest us or complement our skills.

- Human traits are the result of a complex interplay among genetics, environment, how we seek out experiences, and how receptive we are to change as a result of experience.

- Twin studies have shown that the IQs of identical twins are more similar than those of fraternal twins. However, even in identical twins a significant amount of variation in IQ appears to be due to environment.

- Most agree that there is little to no IQ advantage to being born earlier within a family, but there does seem to be an advantage associated with family size. Children from smaller families tend to do a little better on IQ tests. Environmental reasons for this finding may have to do with the increased attention and the added resources that parents with fewer children can provide.

- Estimates regarding how much IQ scores are influenced by genetics vary greatly, with many experts settling on about fifty percent - roughly half of our abilities come from genetics and half from our experiences.

- Such estimates, however, only apply to large groups of people and say nothing about individuals. The interplay between genetics and environment is different in each person. One child may be more open to environmental influences, and another less so.

- Some environmental factors that have been found to enhance IQ are good nutrition and medical care; living in a home with educated parents who provide high-quality language modeling and lots of enrichment activities; good schooling and school attendance; and the presence of a caring and supportive adult who helps the child explore the world and provides instruction in basic skills.

**Other notable books which expand on topics covered in
*Parents' Guide to IQ Testing and Gifted Education:***

Gifted Children; Myths and Realities by Ellen Winner.

> Explores traditional misconceptions about giftedness and
> gifted children.

Frames of Mind: The Theory of Multiple Intelligences by Howard
Gardner.

> The book that introduced the idea of multiple intelligences.

*Magic Trees of the Mind: How to Nurture Your Child's Intelligence,
Creativity, and Healthy Emotions from Birth through Adolescence* by
Marian Diamond and Janet Hopson.

> A look at how a child's abilities can be nurtured through
> early and ongoing environmental experiences.

Misdiagnoses and Dual Diagnosis of Gifted Children and Adults by
James Webb, Edward Amend, Nadia Webb, Jean Goerss, Paul
Beljan, and F. Richard Olenchak.

> Considers similarities between giftedness and such conditions
> as ADHD, mood disorders, Asperger's disorder, Autism, and
> certain emotional problems.

INDEX

I'd like to hear from you...

When I set out to write this book, my goal was to show parents how to recognize signs of giftedness and learning disabilities in their own children and to help them understand how schools use IQ tests and other criteria to select kids for special school programs. I believe I've done this, but I'd like to hear what you think. Did this book answer your questions and help you to find the support your child needs?

Your stories, comments, or ideas on what I can do to make this book more helpful would truly be appreciated. Just visit www.parentguidebooks.com and click on the Contact Us link to let me know what you think.

David Palmer

Additional copies of this book can be ordered by calling: 1-800-247-6553 or through www.parentguidebooks.com

Fast, simple, and secure. Order line open 24 hours a day/7 days a week.